PREACHING

The Art of
Connecting
God and People

PREACHING
The Art of Connecting God and People

F. Dean Lueking

WORD BOOKS
PUBLISHER
WACO, TEXAS

A DIVISION OF
WORD, INCORPORATED

Library of Congress Cataloging in Publication Data

Lueking, F. Dean (Frederick Dean), 1928-
    Preaching: the art of connecting God and people.

    Bibliography: p.
    Includes index.
    1. Preaching. I. Title.
BV4211.2.L78 1985   251   85-17901
ISBN 0-8499-0480-3

567898 FG 987654321

Printed in the United States of America

For
Martin E. Marty

. . . you show that you are a letter from Christ . . . written not with ink but with the Spirit of the living God (2 Cor. 3:3).

Contents

Foreword

In three decades of preaching, reading about preaching, and talking with preachers, I have yet to come across a full length treatment of the subject of this book: people in preaching. I keep finding preachers who are aware of the subject, who agree with its importance, and who join me in the conviction that a book on this aspect of preaching is necessary and timely. But I haven't found the subject opened up. Hence I have written this book.

People within and beyond the congregation are not only listeners, critics, or suggesters, but are essential to preaching itself. Jesus taught emphatically that hearers are to be doers of the Word. They are the "meat" of the message, the mirrors of the truth proclaimed. The people who gather in faith are not only those to whom the truth is told; their lives in response to the truth are part and parcel of preaching.

This is not a book containing sermon illustrations. There is not a story in this book that another preacher needs to borrow or should feel called upon to tell. Rather, the aim of the book is to help the preacher see the incomparable wealth of meaning that is found in the congregation itself and in the community beyond. It seeks to demonstrate the art of weaving that personal richness into sermons. Such an art is rooted in something deeper than homiletical technique. It involves the quality of faith, hope, and love in the whole range of relationships between preacher and people. As those relationships deepen, the one who preaches sees biblical truth proclaimed coming through in the lives of faithful men and women and gives that witness back to the congregation in preaching. In a real sense, then, people *are* sermons, not only hearers of sermons.

As thoughtful readers think about the main point of this book, one issue will probably arise immediately—that of confidentiality.

All who preach regularly, especially in a congregational setting, are called to the utmost integrity when it comes to any sermonic use of the experiences of those they serve. I was talking this point over with a friend when preparing to write the book. He asked me point blank: "In your years of preaching, how often has some member complained that you have broken some confidence, or some other member cautioned lest you do so?" I could answer, "Not once." I owe that witness to readers. If I could not have answered thus, I have no business writing this book and readers would have no reason to continue. It is crucial to keep faith with all who are willing to entrust themselves to preachers in the full vulnerability of their lives. I regard it so, and seek to touch upon this subject from various aspects throughout the book.

I am aware of another reason for preachers to attend more and more faithfully and imaginatively to the people in the congregation as enriching and vital in the contrapuntal dialogue between the biblical text and life in the world. It is the problem of lying. The temptation constantly hovers over and around preachers to come across some spectacular story out of another's experience and offer it as one's own. Over thirty years ago I sat in a congregation and heard a man spellbind his audience with a gripping story he claimed had happened to him in the course of his pastoral work. Less than a month before I had read that story in a book of sermons by Paul Scherer and have wondered ever since what would have been lost by the simple honesty of giving credit to the right person.

Even more damaging was a recent event during a conference on preaching at a prominent divinity school. The evening speaker had not heard the morning lecturer. He fell into this old trap, offering an elaborate story of an experience as though it had been his own. Everyone in the lecture hall realized by the third sentence that the story had been repeated verbatim earlier in the day by a person who was honest enough to authenticate its source. Of course the second speaker lost his credibility and deservedly so.

Why do preachers sometimes falsify in this unethical manner? One main reason is the blindness to the richest source of stories that communicate effectively: the lives of the people themselves who hear and do the truth. This book is an appeal to see how unnecessary it is to overreach the boundaries of integrity as well as propriety.

By no means do I write these pages assuming that people who preach, blunder regularly into the breach of confidentiality from the pulpit or succumb to falsifying the stories of others' experiences by claiming them as their own. My main motive in writing on people in preaching is a desire to share what has been given to me for the good of the larger community of preachers from whom I have also learned so much. I read every sermon I can and gladly hear preaching when the opportunity arises. Over the years I have endeavored to keep up my reading of books of sermons and books on preaching. In recent years I have read sermons from preachers around the country in connection with editing a published series of sermons. What strikes me is the infrequency of references to people in the congregation as mirrors of the text. The great majority of sermons coming across my desk do not incarnate the textual themes in the lives of those who demonstrate both the promise and the struggle of doing the truth. Perhaps preachers conclude much too quickly that reference to individuals in their congregations makes preaching less useful for a wider audience. It is more likely, however, that they do not realize the treasure of people in preaching.

Whatever the cause, this book is an effort toward filling a major gap in the published thought on preaching today.

I am aware of a lively and helpful emphasis in recent years on *story* in preaching and *narrative* in theology. Fred Craddock and Edmund Steimle have helped me see the essential ingredient of story in the biblical revelation of God, and from them I have learned to think more critically about the hermeneutical questions which cluster around the marvel and mystery of how preaching connects God and people.

The more technical aspects of the hermeneutical task in theology and preaching as story have been clarified for me through the writings of James Wiggins and Johannes Metz. Michael Goldberg has taught me the historical context of the concerns that are particular for this strand of religious thought. And no writing on the larger subject of story in preaching and religion is complete without generous attention to Jews, who do it best and have been doing it longest. Jakob Petuchowski's anthologies of rabbinic stories belong in all our libraries as a demonstration of the genius of the Jewish tradition for telling a brief, illuminating story that lets the truth of a biblical text open up afresh.

With due credit to the gifted people who treat the story side of preaching and doing theology, I still look in vain to find the singular emphasis that this book makes. I have striven to digest the major import of the theologians of story in getting at my distinctive point: seeing the lives of congregation members as story, told over a sustained period of time and in the context of close and continuing preacher-to-people relationships.

I also want to pay tribute to those who were my teachers in preaching in earlier days. The most influential teacher I have had in my education for ministry was Richard Caemmerer, of Concordia Seminary and, later, Christ-Seminary, Seminex. His recent death in St. Louis, Missouri, made me think of the extraordinary influence his theology has had on my life and on so many others who preach. His basis for preaching never veered from the "goal-malady-means" construct he set before us with such skill and passion. He led us to foundations which are centered in Christ's saving work witnessed in the biblical gospel. Preaching, Caemmerer taught us, was "offering God." That basis undergirds my preaching and writing on preaching over the past three decades. Whatever I can offer in this volume is based on those foundations I have received and have never found wanting.

Finally and foremost, I acknowledge my indebtedness to those who are the most important source of continuing education in preaching for preachers—the people of the congregation. Since my ordination in the mid-1950s I have served in one congregation. What has been my blessing, and sometimes their burden, is to journey together in faith as a preacher who has known fathers and mothers, sons and daughters, and now a third generation in some instances. Our congregation is named Grace, and well it is named. Grace is what calls and keeps us together; grace is what keeps on giving us the lively Word to preach; grace is what gives me those who demonstrate what makes this book possible and necessary—people in preaching.

F. Dean Lueking
Grace Lutheran Church
River Forest, Illinois

PREACHING
The Art of
Connecting
God and People

▸1◂

About People in Preaching

IN NORTH AMERICA TODAY SOME 350,000 OR MORE men and women preach regularly to congregations. We are but one part of the company of those called to preach throughout the world. In spite of secularizing forces, the shrinking listening span, and increasingly crowded minds of our congregations, preaching goes on. Oral communication has seldom been more important or promising than now. Yet, for all of us who take our cue from the biblical message, the fact remains that what we preach is a God-given "foolishness." St. Paul's term for it (1 Cor. 1:21) is not all that can be said of it, but it remains permanently true. The gospel is a stumbling block to the mind not yet opened to Christ. When it comes to all the other ways whereby humans seek religious experience and some kind of inner illumination, preaching the gospel is a folly and a puzzle. In our generation so given to the visual imagery of television, so conditioned to rate religious talkers by their on-camera sensationalism, so ready to settle for entertainment in religion instead of repentance and costly discipleship, preaching may look like an endangered species. But it's not going to disappear. Faith comes by hearing: "How are they to hear without a preacher?" (Rom. 10:14). Preaching has a future because of the gospel that is to be preached.

The problem is not preaching, but faithless rambling about religion, catering to whatever spiritual fad is current, or tired talk about the Bible that never gets hearers out of the first century. Such is not preaching. Preaching is witnessing to the mighty works of God. It proceeds on the conviction that he has put his saving power into a Word that can be spoken. That Word is centered in Jesus Christ, crucified and risen. The Word is for people, not as a moralizing harangue, not as a specious argument, but as good news for sinners. Preaching has a future because God is who he is for the world in Jesus Christ.

My experience as a preacher in one congregation for thirty years is that all of us who preach need encouragement and correction in staying faithfully at the seeming folly which is at the heart of our calling. In and out of season, through and beyond the trends which come and go, the gospel we preach is the power of God. Not only are we lured into habits of nonpreparation or lightweight treatment of towering biblical texts, we are prone to overlook the abundant resource that people themselves provide for preaching. We need to be able to see again and again the handiwork of the Holy Spirit in the lives of people who hear and do the Word we proclaim, and give those lives a voice in preaching. Preachers, I find as one of them, need to come freshly attentive to the incomparable drama of Christ alive in those who seem on the surface to be only ordinary people.

I have a favorite reference point for this assertion. It has to do with a decision with which everyone in the pastoral calling is familiar. Should the invitation to attend the reception supper after the wedding be accepted or not? Sometimes there are two or three weddings on a fine summer Saturday. Go to one? Hopscotch to several? Or go straight home after a full Saturday, kick off one's shoes after supper and find a quiet corner to think and pray about what is to be preached the next morning?

In thirty years of facing that happy problem in the congregation I serve, my wife and I have decided 99 percent of the time to go when people say come. We have yet to come home from a reception supper grumbling about it. More often than not I come home refreshed by the contact with people at a happy time in their lives, though as the years move along we get home earlier because rest is more necessary. Here is an experience of what being with people at a wedding reception can mean for preaching.

The woman sitting next to me at the supper table was so quiet at first I didn't know whether she wanted to talk at all. But since her son was the groom—(he was marrying one of our members)—she did begin to open up by the time dessert was coming around. Bit by bit she unfolded her story behind this happy day in her life. She was one of twins, born in Latvia in the late 1930s. She remembers, as a five-year-old child, the sight of her father being hustled out of the living room by enemy soldiers who had burst in on them. She saw her father shot to death against the outside wall of the family house.

Then she and her twin sister, her mother, and grandmother were taken off to a detention camp far away. Her grandmother froze to death the first winter, and in the following spring her mother died of malnutrition. The two orphans were cared for somehow by other families who shared their woes as refugees. A year or so later the two children wandered away from the detention camp unheeded, and were taken in by a family that simply gathered them in from the village roadway down which they were walking hand in hand—looking for some human face to receive them.

After a year there, the girls were separated. My supper conversationalist told me of the long, wandering way she followed as a child in her early teens—to Afghanistan and then to India for a time, and finally to the United States. Here she met a fellow Latvian in his final term of medical school study. They were married; he entered his practice. One month after their son was born, the young doctor died of a heart ailment. Over the past twenty-eight years she has worked in a hospital, supporting herself and her young son.

She recalled getting up at 4:30 A.M. instead of the usual 5:30 to go with her boy when he was a teenage ice hockey aspirant. She had helped him through school, and rejoiced in his falling in love. And now came the day when she watched with a full heart as he joined his bride at our altar. All this she was telling me during and after dessert! Before long she would be going home to a now-empty apartment, ready to take up yet one more new chapter in her life.

I recall our mood as my wife and I drove home rather late that Saturday evening. We were quiet, knowing that we had been in the presence of a person of awesome spiritual stature and astounding durability. Here was an extraordinary life experience grounded in the Word of Christ who places us on the resurrection side of every cross. One person, sitting across the wedding supper table, can be and in this case was the equivalent of any number of well-done books and articles on the preaching of the gospel. It is not that those sources are *less*. They are just *other*. They belong with and under the life experiences of people such as the one I've described.

Be sure that this person's quiet story, told not in one gushing account but almost coaxed out, found its way into a later sermon I preached. Transmitting that remarkable testimony, which I could have missed so easily by going home from the wedding or never paying attention to this quiet mother at the reception, gives me a perspective on what I call my problems, and helps others who hear my preaching do the same.

A further footnote on wedding receptions: they have also been occasions when people have had to amble by the table and tell me what "a terrific prayer you gave there, Padre!"

Wedding receptions are also favorite times to see much-loved parishioners with their own families and circles of friends. I always feel I know a family in a new and deeper way after meeting those whom they include in one of life's high moments.

One doesn't go to such occasions with a notepad in hand as if to a research project. One goes to enjoy, to participate (dancing a polka wearing a clerical collar brings either stares or grins), to laugh and converse and—yes—to pray, once the wedding guests can be coaxed into a modicum of quiet so the prayer does not have to be shouted to God above the din of music and the clink of salad forks. But the wedding reception is also a time for absorbing, for listening and seeing, for being in the presence of people whose lives have meaning for preaching.

So much can be learned from people in any informal setting by the simple act of being genuinely interested in them and the stories which reveal something of who they really are behind the façade of surface pleasantries. After enough routine conversation has occurred to give one confidence that the timing is right for questions which can lead to things that truly matter, there are ways to make that shift. A friend of mine has taught me to ask, not "What do you do for a living?" but "Tell me three things I need to know about you to know you." It is revealing that people are so rarely invited to respond to that kind of invitation, and how readily they warm to it once given the chance. When sitting alongside a person with no apparent religious connection I have sometimes asked, "What do you see about religion in the world today that I as a preacher might be missing?"

In response to that inquiry a man once let loose a floodgate of emotion he had been holding back. He told me that his brother had committed suicide some forty years earlier. He was a child at the time, but remembered the pain of that trauma in the family and the greater pain of the local pastor, who refused to conduct the funeral service for the deceased. He wanted me to know that "religion didn't do a damn thing" for his family in its moment of deepest need. He then asked me what I do in such situations, and when learning that the answer was that I minister to the people with the truth and grace of God, he went on to speak of the deep wound that had stayed with him all these years.

Some six months later, I received a phone call while at breakfast at home. A voice asked why I wasn't out working already, especially among folks who have been sore at the church for forty years or more. I recognized my caller's voice immediately. He told me that the chance conversation a half year before had begun new thoughts and directions. In fact he had begun to pray and worship with a congregation again (but not of my denomination, he made it plain!) in the city where he lived. His purpose in calling was to express thanks for a conversation that got beyond the surface to a festering need in his life. My response was to thank him for letting me in on the workings of the Spirit in his life, and the way a simple question led to things that count.

Preaching barren of reference to people is preaching that is critically deficient. If, time after time, in the pulpit or wherever the setting, the biblical Word has no sermon connection with the lives of people who are on the receiving side of it, the Spirit's work is hampered in a major way. Then preaching has taken on the nature of reciting Bible passages or handing on dogmatic summaries of them. A phonograph record can do that.

Preaching that is devoid of human experience is a symptom of limited vision. It marks the absence of perception of what takes place as Word and people intersect. Preaching unconnected to people is like a blueprint without building materials. It is in trouble. It hovers over and around life but does not come all the way to the human situation. This book is a plea to avoid such pitfalls.

It is also a protest against preaching that is a display of how much more widely read the preacher is than those who hear. To be sure, the wealth of the literature of the ages is an abundant source from which the preacher can draw. But sound minds don't have to drop allusions; they have internalized the substantial point and can share it without showing off in the pulpit.

The problem appears in sermon references I have heard and read which presume that people have the time to read book after book that fits into the preacher's list of references. "As Frau Chauchat retorted to Joachim in Thomas Mann's *The Magic Mountain* . . ." is the kind of start-up sentence in a sermon that signals trouble. It imparts the impression that the one in the pulpit wants the hearers to be impressed with his having read Thomas Mann, rather than with whatever it was that the Frau said to Joachim. Such extensive literary references, sprinkled upon preaching like name-dropping, are too borrowed, too much of an adornment. People are left hanging, or quietly defeated by the impression, "What a widely read preacher!" or "What a dolt I am."

It is my sense as I read a fairly sizeable number of sermons each year that this problem was more acute among the pulpit princes of generations ago than at the present time. Yet the problem can and does still afflict us. Literary reference is useful only if it is accessible, conforms naturally with the textual point at hand, and does not require undue time in setting the literary context for the hearer. Showing off with a dazzling exhibition of how much time the preacher spends with

classic and not-so-classic literature is snobbery. It is an offering
of stones to people seeking bread.

Preaching is for people, and the preacher must be with people to reach and relate to them effectively. The goal is to
incorporate people into the preached Word, to give a voice
to the hopes and fears, the victories and defeats that are part
of the journey of faith we all know.

What underlies such integrating and incorporating of people
into the acts of preaching?

First, it is a reflection of love. Drawing upon the lived experiences of young and old, seasoned and novice, fascinating and
ordinary people with whom one shares the daily rounds of
life in a congregation reveals relationships of the kind that
divine love brings about. When people are loved with a Christ-
given love, there is an interest in them, an eye for their significance, a being *for* them no matter what.

Recently I found some evening time to phone people I have
not seen in church for too long. One of those I called told
me why she hadn't come or contacted the church even though
she is going through a time of deepest fear and hurt. She
said she didn't feel as though she deserved help since she
and her husband and family have been absent so long. But
then she went on to the real issue holding her back: "If you
really knew us, Pastor, I don't know how you could love
us. . . ." That speaks for so much in the human heart that
backs away from the power of divine love. Since one doesn't
deserve it, one cannot ask for it.

But the very act of making that call, of listening, of inviting
partners in a crumbling marriage to come in and work at problems with new energies and insight, is an act of love. Again
and again this attitude surfaces: I don't deserve it and therefore
if there is such a thing as grace it's not for me. But this couple,
like so many other people in every imaginable circumstance
of human need, are beginning to face the desolation in their
lives from the perspective of the love that bears, believes,
hopes, and endures all things.

This is the essential force which unites preacher and people,
and which enables the one preaching to rejoice in, struggle
for, offer admonition to, and stay with people through thick
and thin. It is a reflection of love which people have for the

preacher. So often the deeper layers of powerful experiences in Christian living are not laid open to view except in an atmosphere of mutual trust. People who are loved are people who trust. The extent to which the experience of people emerges more and more effectively in preaching is the measure of the extent and growth of love that opens people up to each other. Love provides the only right motive for the act of preaching itself. It is the power which moves the one who preaches out among people with care for the uniqueness of every human. It quickly shows in the manner as well as the content of preaching. The difference between preaching *at* people and preaching *for* people is the difference that love makes. It is at the very heart of integrating people into the act of preaching.

Incorporating people into preaching is the mark of respect for those who listen to preaching and who give so much to the preacher by their intensive listening. Relatively few baptized Christians get up every morning and go into the day with a sense of "Let's see; what do I have to offer today in my life that will become preachable?" The majority of us underestimate the significance of our days and deeds. By respect for people I mean the quality of remaining teachable by people, and doing what the basic meaning of respect is— "looking again."

To *re-spectare*, to look a second time at a tiny or large segment of a person's life, is to see that to which the person herself may be oblivious. The preacher re-spects, has an eye for the meaning under the apparently humdrum. Time and again the preacher is side by side with those who have borne with an alcoholic partner for years, who have cared for an aged parent, who have put up with an impossible boss, who have sacrificed for employees, who have gone against the tide of campus trendiness. Looking again at such people is more than a matter of manners. It is seeing in their lives more than they may see. Preaching calls for such vision, which is the essence of respect.

Incorporating people into preaching is a mark of faith. It is a sign of the conviction that people are not only what they are now, but are on their way toward becoming the full persons God means them to be. Relating the experiences of people in preaching is the evidence of the conviction that Christ, the Son of God, is indeed incarnate. He is there with his Spirit in people, even in the least of them. He is there with power to move people toward the fuller stature of his grace.

"Inasmuch as you have done it to the least of these"—the stranger welcomed, the naked clothed, the sick and imprisoned visited and cared for in the parable of Jesus in Matthew 25—the action of faith is being *told.* That does not happen in heaven but on earth. It happens not in the abstraction of life but in its concreteness.

C. S. Lewis wrote that next to the Blessed Sacrament itself, the most sacred thing presented to our senses is our neighbor, and particularly if that neighbor is one in Christ. Truly in him and her Christ lies hidden.[1] When that faith is active, preaching shows it.

There is another aspect of this essential practice of incorporating people into Christian proclamation. The preacher needs the strength of faith because there are times when we do not want such specific reference. Sometimes we prefer a bland generality to a pointed, personal illustration of the force of sin in human life. A collision occurs when the unregenerate pockets left in our baptized life offer resistance to preaching. The hearer makes the connection with the Word of divine judgment and personal experience. That is never anything less than a painful, head-to-head confrontation.

One ventures into this realm with fear and trembling. At a time when the black ghetto in the city in which I live was literally on fire, and when suburban fears and flight were nearing peak proportions, I spoke in a sermon of a person who resented the sight of black Christians walking into white homes for an evening of Bible study while the rocks and flames were flying. It was my calling not only to speak of our inter-parish network of biracial Christians that had come into being and was continuing in spite of the atmosphere of violence and fear. In that sermon I had also to testify against the sin of resentment and resistance to the Spirit of Christ. To lift up the weakness of faith in the experience of phone-callers and note-writers who said, "Cool it, Pastor," became an act of faith.

I believe that people can and do repent of sin, but this

comes only through that wrenching and death-dealing experience of the law of God convicting the heart of sin. Preaching that judgment in the reality of prejudiced attitudes and biased actions is the responsibility of biblical preaching. That more phone calls followed and some torn-up offering envelopes appeared in the collection plates on Sunday is only a small price for preaching the Word in the fullness of the faith.

Relating preaching and people is like the job of a construction worker whose hand is on the lever that detonates dynamite at the other end of the long fuse line. I find such moments in preaching very difficult, and I am suspicious if anyone delights in them. But when human experience is incorporated into preaching and set forth as "our experience," "our sin," "our irresponsibility and unfaithfulness," it is proclaiming the word of faith, not just thwacking people. It is the good fight of faith, commonly shared in judgment as well as in grace.

The integration of people into preaching is the fruit of experience. How long does it take for a preacher to be in a congregation until the life of the people is vivid in his own awareness? There is no single answer. One person can preach for hardly a year in a parish and already be gifted in the art of incorporating people into preaching. Another can be present for ten or forty years in the same congregation and still the unpeopled sermons drone on. It is necessary to have time with people.

In my first month of ordained ministry I called on a hospitalized parishioner; he had a heart ailment. My overlong visit with him, marked by an overview of the whole history of salvation, nearly gave him a relapse. At a later time when he was back to health he helped me appreciate the value of a one-sentence prayer and the simple act of placing my hand in his. One learns with time and grace.

What one learns is the great patience and forbearing love that laity shower upon clergy. Surely all of us who preach experience this grace. People teach us so much of what we know about ministry. The congregation is the primary classroom of our continued learning and growth after the seminary. The longer view of God's unhurried ways with his people takes time for us all to absorb. There are no shortcuts.

One of the benefits of being in one parish over a long period of time is the gift of seeing the Word at work in youth who

grow up to become parents who have their own youth to
nurture. But those just beginning in ministry can see it from
their earliest days of service. The experience factor is not tied
to being at one place. It has to do with loving, believing,
respecting and being with people, whether the time is short
or long.

The incorporation of people into preaching must share this
aspect with all the rest of sound preaching: it is invitational.
It is a calling out to people through people, an offering to
people in a way that summons men and women to love God,
fellow humans, and themselves. Weaving the experiences of
people into preaching is not a bypath, an "illustration" that
entertains or diverts from the main point. It is an essential
part of the proclamation itself. It deserves to be done with
passion in preaching, as evidence of the genuineness of the
preacher's concern that hearers see the truth of God located
in human life here and now.

A passionate urgency about this need not sink into despera-
tion or overdoing the point. It is to be proclaimed with an
awareness that neither preachers nor hearers have forever in
our obedience of faith. Here are people who exhibit that imme-
diacy of faith active in love. The point of speaking about
them is that their lives speak to us. Their experiences move
and bless us. This is the sense of invitation that the marvelous
mercy of God extends. Christ's grace reaches others through
those whose very lives are an invitation to taste and see that
the Lord is good.

Finally, the function of incorporating people into preaching
is an expression of what the purpose of preaching is. A passage
from St. Paul in Ephesians 4 is one of the key New Testament
references. God has called apostles, prophets, evangelists, pastors, and teachers, "in order that his people be equipped for
serving . . ." (Eph. 4:11–13). Preaching without reference to
the faith experience of people infers that faith and experience
do not connect. But the faithful and artful weaving of Christian life into the proclamation is already evidence that the
connecting is going on. There they are and there is their testimony! See them and hear of the faithfulness of the struggle
toward faith in such a way as to be enlightened and uplifted
by the Spirit's work.

Preaching is equipping. The miracle that is in and with and under preaching is this: God is pleased to place his power to make all things new in the fragile and fallible human instrument of human speaking. In the witness that reaches back to the revelation of his grace and judgment through the patriarchs and prophets, and supremely through his coming to us in the birth and ministry, the death and resurrection of Jesus Christ, God claims us wayward ones as beloved, forgiven children. The Spirit whom God sends in the Savior's name is the Lord and Giver of life, we say in the Nicene Creed. This life is imparted in faithful speaking which links people to the grace of God and equips them to live out the life that is ever new in the hope and promise of the gospel.

When preachers hear a parishioner say at the church door: "That was a good sermon," they are glad but they know that it is too early to tell if the living Word has found its mark. What follows preaching is the work of the Word that issues in attitudes, decisions, and deeds in the particular life situation of that person following the hearing of the Word.

These themes are all gathered around a set of basics. Preaching is an act of witness to the God who is forever bound up with people. Preachers are themselves messengers. Those who are called to proclaim are with and among people, and the links that hold both together are the bonds of love and faith. The message is about God—the God who joins his name with people's names: Abraham, Isaac, and Jacob—the Father of our Lord Jesus Christ. The purpose of such preaching is to offer God to people so that all may belong to him and see the truth alive in others. Strong biblical themes underlie all this. To that we now turn.

▶2◀

People in the Biblical Story

THE BIBLE IS THE RECORD NOT OF THE HUMAN search for God but of God's search for those he made in his image.

The biblical story is the witness to the sovereign Creator who made all things and who will not leave us to the consequences of our own sin, but who ceaselessly comes to us and every generation to reclaim us as his own.

Our God is the God of Abraham, Isaac, and Jacob, the God who joins his name with the names of people. As he entered into human history in a unique way with his saving acts, he covenanted with a person. This man was at home in Ur of the Chaldees. To Abram, as he was originally called, God revealed his covenant of mercy for the ages to come. With Sarai his wife, he was led to the new land of Canaan to a specific people—the heirs of Abraham. The new name signifies the formation of a people, indeed the formation of a multitude of peoples who would come to know the goodness of the Lord (Gen. 17:5).

What follows in the biblical record is the story of people—individuals, families, friends, enemies, communities, clans, and, after the release from the long years of slavery in Egypt, the formation of a nation of Israel.

It is people whom we meet through the pages of the Torah, the books of Moses—people with faces and names and hopes and dreams, with greed and idolatry, with tragedy and suffering, with courage and faithfulness. The Bible is decidedly different from the sacred writings of the Upanishads or the mantras and sutras of the Buddhist religious tradition. The Bible never takes its focus off God dealing with people, with individuals and communities that are always specific and particular. The destiny of these few who are chosen out of the many provides the clue to God's gracious intentions for the entire family of humankind.

Sarai laughs at the announcement of her impending motherhood when she is already wrinkled with age. But the Sarai who laughed in unbelief becomes Sarah, the mother of Isaac, through whom the promise of the covenant is continued (Gen. 18).

Abraham hears of the Lord's judgment upon the decadence of Sodom. Through his pleading to God for that hopeless place on the eastern shore of the Dead Sea, it turns out that the presence of ten righteous persons is the basis for the divine decision to show mercy. Through a few, God acts with mercy for many (Gen. 18:22–33).

The life of Abraham's son, Isaac, is called for as a testing of Abraham's faith. That son is given back to a faithful father, who on a lonely mountain was ready to part with his only heir, the son of the covenantal promise. This momentous hinge point in the early history of God's people involves a particular experience in the life of a father with a son offered and received back again in faith (Gen. 22:1–18).

Isaac meets Rebekah by a waterspring and is drawn by her beauty and gracefulness. Another story centered around a family unfolds (Gen. 24), with twin sons born to the couple who had been childless (Gen. 25:21).

Then follows the drama of Isaac and Rebekah's sons, Jacob and Esau, with no details spared of the chicanery of the former and the hard lot of the latter. Jacob, with all his humanity held up to the light of the biblical record, is nevertheless the bearer of the promise, the all-too-fallible witness to the supreme truth that God keeps on calling and working his will through human beings (Gen. 27–31). This Jacob is given the name Israel, based upon one fateful night of wrestling with God through his messenger (Gen. 32).

The sons given to Jacob and Rachel are the people who

plot to do away with the favored younger brother, Joseph. At age seventeen he is assaulted in the field and sold to a passing caravan to Egypt where he rises to a position of prominence in the court of Pharaoh (Gen. 37–41). His deeds of prudence in the time of plenty lay the basis for his acts of mercy in the years of famine. In the midst of that extremity the beautiful story of reconciliation is told with all its dramatic pathos and the underlying theme of divine mercy interwoven in the events of a family brought together again (Gen. 42–47).

Look at the person-centered nature of the biblical account as it takes us through the life experiences of a chosen people: a call to journey from Ur to Canaan; an aged couple stumbling in the face of a promise of an heir; that heir taken from the brink of death and sustaining the covenantal promise; love at first sight; treachery in a remote field; the rise to leadership in a foreign land; the triumph of forgiveness over malice; and the reunion of a quarrelsome family. Listing the events, even in this abbreviated form, underlines the particular way that God speaks his word of truth to the world in the first book of the Bible. It is people with names and faces and experiences of all sorts who come before our eyes.

The same characteristic continues throughout the Old Testament. In the devotional writings of the Hebrew Scriptures, particularly the Psalms, we meet the full range of human emotions: joy and praise, thanksgiving and peaceful reflection upon God's goodness, anger and impatience with God and people, despair and heartache, repentance and renewal. The book of Job sets forth the mystery of God's ways in the midst of pain and suffering, an elemental issue in every human life. In the book of Ruth the depth of human affection finds its expression in the gentle devotion of Ruth for Boaz. The Song of Songs is a celebration of the sensuality and passionate love which humans share. Doubt and skepticism are prominent themes in Ecclesiastes, and in the books of Ezra, 1 Chronicles, and 2 Chronicles the careful reader picks out the contours of defensiveness and authoritarianism. All these books are rooted in the experience of people to whom God comes and with whom God works.

The books of the prophets are unique in the whole of

religious literature. Their distinctiveness comes through the channels of particular faithful and courageous individuals who rise up on the landscape of Israel's life, who receive and deliver the Word of divine judgment upon Israel's sins and who also offer the promise of God's redeeming love as the ultimate hope to which his people must cling.

The prophets do not mutter in isolation. Amos leaves his remote village of Tekoa, south of Bethlehem, and journeys north to raise hob with the idolaters at Bethel. For three years Isaiah devotes his keen intellect and conscience to the grievous inequities of the southern kingdom of Judah in which he lived. He also marches naked and barefoot through the streets of Jerusalem as a sign of the slavery and exile coming upon a people mired in a way of life that scorned the justice of God (Isa. 20:1–6).

Jeremiah, that prophet who more than any other revealed in his own tempestuous heart the plight of the people, is beaten and thrown into a dungeon on the charge of treason for his prophetic Word of judgment upon the entrenched self-interests that were eating away at the integrity of the people of God in his day (Jer. 37:11 ff.).

What the prophets never tired of proclaiming was the specific nature of the sins of the people, particularly against the poor and disinherited of the land. They lifted up the plight of the oppressed and called for justice in the marketplace, for righteousness in all human dealings, for truth to have its home in the heart. Isaiah's opening words set the tone:

> Wash yourselves, make yourselves clean; remove the evil of your doings from before my eyes; cease to do evil, learn to do good; seek justice, correct oppression; defend the fatherless, plead for the widow (1:16–17).

For those who respond to Jesus as the messianic Lord to whom all the Torah, the Writings, and the Prophets bear witness, the New Testament Scriptures bring the revelation of God to bear upon a certain One born in Bethlehem. Although the New Testament Gospels never intend to be complete biographies of all that Jesus did and said, each Gospel proclaims his words and deeds among people in all conditions of life.

It all leads to his cross and death at Calvary outside Jerusalem's gates. There he lays down his life in the sovereign freedom of divine love for the world.

His resurrection on the third day is told in the setting of unbelieving disciples who first took care for their own safety behind locked doors. His victory for the whole world is revealed to faithful but mournful women who are the first to be surprised by joy. It is among disciples at their nets that he makes his risen glory known on the Galilean shore, with fish for breakfast (John 21:9–14)!

At the heart of the Good News is this: the eternal Word became flesh, became a living, breathing, fully human being with us and for us (John 1:14). In that single, unrepeatable life, God is pleased to dwell in the fullness of his grace and truth. It is in the face of Jesus, as Paul the apostle wrote to a struggling congregation in Corinth, that the full brightness of the glory of God shines out for all (2 Cor. 4:6).

The new People of God are launched in mission to the world as the Holy Spirit is poured out upon them at the first Pentecost. As Acts 2 describes, those who were deniers and escapees at the darkest moment of Jesus' trial and death, are now proclaimers who have his resurrection deed on their lips and their lives as evidence of God's mercy for sinners. He makes new beginnings for people who had given up on him and themselves.

From place to place, from person to person, the Good News goes. The earliest sermons of the first followers of the Way are anchored in the particulars of the moment and they draw upon the singular mercies of God for people, from Abraham on to the crucified and risen Lord. Peter declares that gospel in the face of accusations that the disciples are drunk with new wine (at 9 A.M.?, his wry, one-line disavowal asks, Acts 2:15). Peter and John speak the gospel with a healed lame man leaping and jumping throughout the temple precincts, in the face of an incensed crowd of priests and Sadducees who would silence them if they could.

Stephen, the first of the new People of God to seal his testimony with his life blood, proclaims the whole litany of God's mighty works of salvation through patriarchs and Moses and finally through his Son, the Righteous One "whom you have now betrayed and murdered" (Acts 7:52). As the uncompromising preaching of the first martyr found its target in the hardened hearts of those who threw it back at him, Saul looked on with approval.

The disturbingly serene and forgiving Stephen supplied the key moment in a fateful inner turning that finally led Saul, the enemy of the Way, to Paul, the proclaimer of the Way. In three eventful missionary journeys to the west, Paul was the messenger to Gentiles as well as Jews. His preaching was grounded in the saving works of God that culminated in Jesus the Christ. The Word that God reconciled people through the grace of His Son was applied to the varied situations of life which the epistles of Paul emphasize. It was people to whom he pointed as "living letters" which testify both to the grace of Christ and to the authenticity of his own ministry:

> You yourselves are our letters of recommendation, written on your hearts, to be known and read by all men; and you show that you are a letter from Christ delivered by us, written not with ink but with the Spirit of the living God, not on tablets of stone but on tablets of human hearts (2 Cor. 3:2–3).

It is the day-by-day life of people in congregations that is set before us throughout the Acts of the Apostles and through the epistles which illumine the ways in which the Word of Christ takes root in human life.

The majestic fullness of the grace of God in Christ Jesus that Paul sets forth in the first eleven chapters of Romans does not end as an abstract treatise on grace, law, and election. He writes as a missionary pastor to "all God's beloved in Rome who are called to be saints" (Rom. 1:6). What follows chapter eleven is the application of the ethical consequences of grace in daily life:

> Let love be genuine; hate what is evil, hold fast to what is good; love one another with brotherly affection; outdo one another in showing honor. Never flag in zeal, be aglow with the Spirit, serve the Lord. Rejoice in your hope, be patient in tribulation, be constant in prayer. Contribute to the needs of the saints, practice hospitality. Bless those who curse you; bless and do not curse them. Rejoice with those who rejoice

and weep with those who weep. Live in harmony with one another; do not be haughty but associate with the lowly; never be conceited. Repay no one evil for evil but take thought for what is noble in the sight of all. If possible, so far as it depends upon you, live peaceably with all (12:9–18).

Before concluding the letter to the congregation in Rome, Paul commends Prisca and Aquila "who risked their necks for my life" and asks that the church that meets in their house be greeted (16:3–4). He names a newcomer, Phoebe, in the ranks of women servants and commends her to the congregation (16:1). He remembers, names personally, and asks special greetings for Epaenetus, Mary, Andronicus and Junias, Ampliatus, Urbanus, Stachys, Apelles, those of the household of Aristobulus, Herodion, and those in the family of Narcissus. With each of these personal references he adds some commendation of their faithfulness as Christians in Rome. Before finishing the closing chapter he adds fifteen more names to the list of people whose devotion and faithfulness he had witnessed. Paul not only greets them all and salutes them with words of encouragement; he adds the greetings of Timothy, Lucius, Jason, and Sosipater, his coworkers in the apostolate, as well as Tertius the scribe of the letter, Gaius who was Paul's host, Erastus the city treasurer (!), and Quartus, another brother in the Lord.

The Epistle of Paul to the Romans is not only the classic Pauline letter plumbing the depths of the mystery of God's revelation in Jesus Christ; it is also the connecting of that profound mystery with the day-to-day ethical contours of the new life in Christ and the personal encouragement to dozens of specific individuals with whom Paul had worshiped and worked in Rome.

In fewer words, but with the same basic pattern of first what God has done in Christ for people and then what that means in the lives of people, the remaining epistles of Paul tell the story of Christ's presence for and in the world. People are always in focus.

Not only does Paul cite the power of the risen Lord in the lives of others; he also lets it show that he is part of the process. Early in the first missionary journey John Mark

left the company of the apostles as they arrived on the main-
land of Asia Minor. There is no explanation. "John left them
and returned to Jerusalem" (Acts 13:13). When it came time
to select companions for the second missionary journey, John
Mark was proposed as a participant (by his cousin, Barnabas),
but Paul would have none of it. "Paul thought it best not
to take with them one who had withdrawn from them in
Pamphylia and had not gone with them to the work" (Acts
15:37–38). The sharp contention that followed resulted in Paul
and Silas going in one direction, and Barnabas and John Mark
following another course. Apostles, too, had tempers and arguments. But much later in his life, after Paul had been seasoned
by a life of discipleship, he wrote a heartening note at the
end of his letter to the Colossian congregation: "Aristarchus
my fellow prisoner greets you, and Mark the cousin of Barnabas [concerning whom you have received instructions—if he
comes to you, receive him]" (Col. 4:10).

Two missionary apostles once at odds were united in common service to a congregation years later. It is not a major
part of New Testament writings. But a seemingly small thing
like Paul's commendation of John Mark to the Colossians is
nonetheless a sign of something very significant taking place.
The missionary teacher is teachable. The great proclaimer of
the divine reconciliation of God with the world is reconcilable
with one brother who for some reason unknown to us left
the work at a critical moment—but came back.

From Abraham's early vision of the astounding destiny God
promised the world, through to the book of Revelation and
the lonely witness of John the exiled apostle to the victory
of God over tyrannies parading so confidently at the time,
people and congregations are inextricably woven into the
story.

Preaching the biblical word today cannot take on a people-
less monotone when such a story of people's stories is its
authority. The Bible itself begs for, enables, provides, and
commands that the truth of God be witnessed in word and
deed by people for people in all their specific circumstances,
gifts, weaknesses, hopes, failures, sin, and forgiveness. Here
is one expression of the mandate for preaching the Life of
God in the lives of people:

Since we are surrounded by so great a cloud of witnesses, let us lay aside every weight, and sin which clings so closely, and let us run with perseverance the race that is set before us, looking to Jesus the pioneer and perfecter of our faith, who for the joy that was set before him endured the cross, despising the shame, and is seated at the right hand of the throne of God (Heb. 12:1–2).

▸ *3* ◂

The Act of Preaching

BIBLICAL PREACHING IS MUCH MORE THAN A string of anecdotes from the lives of people. Sermons which reflect biblical preaching have a coherence that brings together a number of essential elements. The witness of people belongs in this larger context.

One of these elements is preparation for preaching. This takes varied forms. James Glasse speaks for many of us when he says that he does not prepare sermons during the week, rather he prepares himself to preach. That statement has a point easily missed. The sermon is not a disembodied composition worked out so that the preacher finishes off the last sentence with a sigh that the sermon is now over. Some preachers have commendable discipline and hold themselves to the schedule of carefully outlining and then putting a sermon into completed manuscript form before Friday noon every week. Such a regimen is not to be scorned. But for me that format does not work. From all I learn in talking about sermonizing with fellow practitioners, I gather that I am not in the minority. We don't go into the cave on Monday morning and come out at the weekend with the oracle in typed, double-spaced form.

But that's a caricature of a much-needed discipline. My preaching mentor in seminary years made it emphatic that writing out manuscripts is a must. The discipline of putting incompletely formed thoughts and insights onto paper before preaching keeps the preacher more free of clichés and imprecise communication. Over time it leads to greater clarity of thought and expression. Since our calling has to do with words and their creative use, we have no choice but to be careful for language and seek to be at our best so that the Word is heard in our words. Every sermon preached may not have been incubating in written manuscript form. It may be that a preliminary outline followed by an extended outline is the next best thing to a written manuscript. Methods are variable because no two weeks are the same, and no two preachers are identical. But regardless of the variances, all of us have the responsibility to devote ourselves to the hard work of clear communication. It doesn't come automatically. It is the fruit of disciplined thought, study, written, and then spoken expression.

Early weekday mornings are golden spaces for the requisite study and formal preparation for preaching. Textual selection varies among denominational traditions. All my life I have been part of a tradition that is based on particular passages or pericopes for the church year. The longer I live the more I appreciate it. The more I associate with colleagues unfamiliar with this systematic coverage of a very wide spread of biblical truth, the more I find them open to its value. A set system of pericopes stretches the preaching horizon. Accepting a year-round series of prescribed scripture readings which are also part of the worship service itself aids in moving the preacher beyond the circle of favorite parts of the Bible. It leads to more faithful proclamation of the whole counsel of God. Preaching from texts that are heard in the worship service aids in integrating preaching into the wholeness of worship in the gathered congregation.

Clergy support groups are increasingly available to those who preach. One which has particular meaning for me is a Friday morning group that is now in its sixth year in our community. A dozen of us, Protestant and Roman Catholic preachers, meet at 7:30 A.M. for breakfast, followed by a time for intercessory prayer and singing—or sometimes silence for our own petitions to God. Then comes an hour of study of the three biblical texts that are set for ten days hence (thus a week from the coming Sunday). We change off each Friday in the church kitchen locations. Each week one of the group leads worship, and another is responsible to get us into the texts. I find this 7:30–9:30 Friday morning time a continuous stimulation. Practitioners make good teachers. Preachers have much to teach fellow preachers, particularly when our textual study is carried on in the setting of our respective congregational ministries. A visitor looking over our shoulders in these sessions would be hard put to pick out the Methodist, the Catholic, the Presbyterian, the Lutheran. It is revealing how these terms remain adjectives rather than becoming nouns when a group like this is in earnest about wrestling with biblical texts and striving together for meanings that are preachable.

In traveling around the country and keeping in contact with pastors I have puzzled over why such a support group devoted specifically to sermon text preparation seems to be rare. Some have flourished for awhile, but then died out because the focus on preparing to preach specific texts became blurred by too many other interests addressed or too little effort expended by the participants.

What keeps us together year in and year out on a weekly basis are the demands of weekly preaching. Even if only two or three group members are available and interested, the method has value. It is a starter. It sets mental wheels turning on a text ten days before the time of preaching. It provides initial ideas which are then furthered or laid aside as textual study continues.

Perhaps because it is primarily a textual study group for the purpose of preaching, it is also the most effective support group I have ever experienced. As an occasional by-product we find that things deeper inside of us as individuals get a hearing. The trust level is strong. We keep on coming back because we know we are there for each other and for the good of the person who preaches as well as for the sermons we preach.

The text to be preached deserves a place of prominence in the mind of the preacher early in the week. The weekday morning time that is given to preparing myself to preach is much better organized when I know the particular text from which I will be preaching.

Two kinds of specialty books enrich my textual understanding year after year. The first is exemplified by Klaus Westermann's little volume, *A Thousand Years and a Day,* which overviews Old Testament theology. I don't always remember the historical context of a given pericope. It may have been years since I have preached from that book of the Bible. What means so much at this stage of preparing a sermon is a grasp of the larger sweep of the biblical message of which this text is a part.

Walter Brueggemann's *Genesis* is a more recent example of the same kind of welcome assistance that a biblical scholar supplies for the preaching task. Every preacher has a particular set of books on both Testaments of the Bible that keep on delivering help for preaching. We all have commentaries that speak to us. Many of us are subscribers to journals and magazines and ministerial book and tape series which concentrate on Bible and theology.

The circle of help is wider. I subscribe to journals and magazines that have no churchly reference but which offer excellent writing on all aspects of life. Sometimes a thoughtful writer will probe an aspect of the human story directly related to a biblical text. It is good to have all the antennae out that we can possibly manage. The Bible we preach is constantly in dialogue with the world in its witness to God who is in the world and for the world, now and forever.

Morning hours, often spent in reading and study, are followed by afternoon and evening hours; these are for me the richest times for people contact so essential to preaching.

Most of us counsel people. What few who entrust to us their concerns of life realize is the manner in which they open up a text that has, until that moment, been mute. One recent example of this comes to mind. The text coming for Sunday in that week was the Genesis 11 account of the tower of Babel. Verse seven of the story speaks of the consequence of self-serving name-seeking and the refusal to go beyond the clannishness of the proposed tower. Language is confused; one person cannot understand the other. That much seemed clear enough, and my mind was on the barriers that nonunderstood language erects among people. But something deeper lay under that verse; a Brueggemann insight opened it up. The point is not just that people can't make sense of a foreign language they do not know. It hints at the absence of will and the breakdown of desire to understand each other.

That thought was only beginning to stir when an hour's counseling conversation with a person took place on the afternoon of the same day I had been reading the Genesis 11 text. The woman spoke of her experience a year previous. Her husband told her one holiday weekend that he did not love her, had never loved her, and had no intention to ever love her. Some thirty years of marriage, with all the striving to get through, trying to reach the other, trying to communicate love and affection was thrown aside in one devastating conversation. As the woman spoke of the shattering experience of having her husband's determination *not* to communicate dumped on her, I thought of the Genesis 11:7 text. There it is in a person's life! Across the desk from me was one for whom the immense burden of being unheard because of being unloved is a reality. Her experience illuminated the Genesis 11 text about the basic problem of sin that infects all broken-down communication.

That person also knows where help lies, for she has not succumbed to despair. In the subsequent months she has known the care of God in the readiness of people to hear and help. Her prayers have not gone unanswered. Though she was helpless to keep the marriage together, she has found the strength for starting again in a new life, sustained by Christ's grace in her own personhood, confident of her skills for her livelihood, grateful for those close friends who are like an oasis in the loneliest moments, and eager for a place in a new congregation.

In such an hour, a text just studied comes alive. With care for her trust in me shown by her telling me her experience, I used it in a sermon. Her encounter with the shattering force of the refusal to love and to communicate confirmed the text. Often I speak of a text in preparation to a person who is unwittingly opening up its meaning to me. Then the relationship takes a special turn. It is not so much counselor-counselee, but both of us drawing from the biblical text, each of us finding in the Word that which nurtures us both. The best thing to be said about pastoral counseling is that the one seeking counsel is steered to the Word and the Spirit of God at work through the judgment or the grace found there. In such transactions the spiritual core of counseling is established and the dependency upon God of both pastor and the one seeking help is made clear.

Behind the act of preaching each week are moments spent with people in hospitals, sickbeds at home, classrooms, homes for the aged, and—as often as I can—visits with parishioners at their place of work. The weekly rounds include the duties of parish administration, which ranked lowest in interest in my study years of preparation for ordination. I passed by the "how to" books that featured the wizardry of card-index files or the latest on pastoral management by objectives. The trouble was not with the intention of well-meaning authors. What got lost were the people-connections that such tools must have.

Taking an active responsibility for helping a Sunday-school superintendent find teachers tells me important things about Jesus' Parable of the Talents. So does the descent to the boiler room of the church building to share the victory of janitor or trustee in conquering the beast yet one more time. Buildings and their maintenance are part of the whole picture of the weekly rounds.

God help congregations that would have to depend on the preachers to handle the welding torch or cement trowel. But the people who do these things well are among those who contribute toward preaching. Getting beyond the congregation membership in contact with people is an important means for me to realize the congregation is in the world and the world is in the congregation.

More regular opportunities for this kind of people contact come through active membership in civic or other community organizations, where one sees the providence of God at work as well as opposite forces. One pastor can't be everywhere and into everything, of course. But every day and every week means moving in many circles which put preachers side by side with people of marvelous variety and no little talent. These contacts always have potential for preaching, since sermon preparation is going on all the time in all kinds of places inside and outside the congregation, right up to the moment of preaching from the pulpit.

The anchor point for making those weekly rounds significant is finally the text and the gospel to be preached from
that text. The process is one of constant interaction between
the Word and people. The weekly rounds cannot be allowed
to become so engrossing that no time is left for wrestling
one central thought from the text. This can be put into one
sentence as the key to the sermon, that connects God's grace
with a goal of change for the believer's life.

What then follows in my form of sermon preparation is
the writing of a preliminary outline around the central
thought. That can take more than three minutes. When I speak
of a preliminary and then a completed outline, the term means
for me between six and eight distinctive but related points
that can lead over the content I intend the sermon to cover.
Most often that process takes place in my pastoral study.
But it can also happen in a hospital room waiting for a patient
to come down from surgery, between acts at a play, getting
to or from somewhere on a plane or in a car, or when trapped
at a meeting that is going nowhere.

Once an outline is formed I am best helped when I find
somebody with whom to talk it through. In the congregation
I serve, which has a pastoral staff, that person is often my
partner in ministry. I have the blessing of a wife who will
listen and offer useful response. And I cherish the gift of
parishioners who will be at church for something or other
and who will give me their listening time for even five minutes.
Just to talk it through with someone is an act that in itself
is clarifying. Does this point make sense? Does that point
actually support the main theme? Is my assessment of something truly significant about the text or its relation to life
confirmed in another's estimate of it? Is there fluff in the shape
of the sermon so far? These are questions to which I welcome
candid answers. I find that people are not imposed upon by
such brief conversations. More often than not, people who
help me at that stage of preparation are themselves helped
to hear the sermon more effectively when it is preached.

Easiest to overlook or bypass in this process of study, obser-
vation, integration of experience, outlining and writing, and
finally the preaching of the sermon itself, is the groundwork
of prayer. I admire those who are more disciplined or more

gifted in this essential than I. In my own experience, "arrow" prayers dominate. A sentence of petition as a textual study is begun, more words of prayer for clarity and persuasiveness as the week goes along and the sermon continues to build. Prayer before worship begins, prayer before the first pulpit sentence is uttered, prayer following worship, prayer at the end of the day—these are occasions for God to be sought, thanked, and depended upon for preaching.

No doubt hearers can perceive whether preaching is integrated with prayer. The difference becomes clear when the act of preaching is witness to God and an offer of Christ or something else: pulpit oration, recitation of Bible passages, pontificating on current events, or preacher vanity. Preaching can only become the lifeline of the risen Lord to his people as the one preaching is alive to prayer and grateful for its power. The Word is not ours but God's. The power whereby preaching becomes faith-giving and life-sustaining is that of the Holy Spirit. Happy is the preacher who banks all on that truth.

The act of preaching is—for me—both the main course and dessert of the ministry. My circumstances may be unique, but the interior dynamic of what happens in preaching is one that all of us share. It is an astounding privilege—in fact so momentous that one can only begin to grasp it. Think of it: a congregation of believers calls one into their midst to say aloud what God intends all to have in his Word!

What happens as conversation moves to proclamation is evident in my experience of meeting with a bereaved family prior to preaching the funeral sermon. I knew the deceased only slightly, the widow somewhat more. Both were people of unusual qualities. Neither had much connection with any congregation. Sitting in the living room of the family the evening before, I found the atmosphere formal and understandably limiting. The people present were still under the shock of death. It was not their custom to be chatty about anything. What does one do in such a situation after gathering the necessary obituary information? Not much, and a decently prompt exit is a favor to them as well as a certain relief for me. But these people are Christians, and even though unpracticed in parish worship, ready for preaching the next day.

At the funeral itself, my calling as a preacher is not to eulogize, to judge, to play God, to bring warm fuzzies, or to pretend that I knew all the fullness of this man's life. My calling is that of a witness, a herald, a bringer of Christ's grace and peace to hearts that are ready. In those moments of preaching something happens that I cannot adequately describe. People hear with a kind of openness and receptivity that is just not there in the living room setting the previous evening. Nor can that readiness be commandeered. It is given.

People receive Christ as Bread for the soul and feed upon him. Preachers know, at least most of the time, when that kind of faithful listening happens. The experience is awesome, as all who share in preaching are often reminded.

The act of preaching, which needs so much energy and time and grace in preparation, offers moments that are not possible to predict and can never be taken for granted. There are times in preaching when the listening is so intense as to be almost palpable. These moments are not all that plentiful, nor do they signify the only times when preaching is effective.

It is revealing when preachers learn that people can respond more readily to what might seem a minor point in a sermon. People hear, of course, in connection with needs, sensitivities, and anticipations. There is something of a mystery in the way that a truth can lay hold on a hearer's mind and heart to the exclusion of all else that the one preaching thought was more important. As experience with people grows, it happens increasingly that the sight of some person whose gifts or experience or need is known will lead to a much more concentrated speaking to a point. That is why preaching several times on a Sunday morning never means preaching a sermon exactly the same way. As one's eye meets another's, as this preacher's mind is meshed with that person's urgent situation, outlined points can be shuffled on the spot.

From time to time there is good room for laughter by preacher and hearers. I find that the temptation to build in humorous stories is best resisted. It is better that out of the spontaneity of the moment some word can come through that invites people to smile out loud. The notion that such is never proper in worship does not come from the Scriptures. Of course people who rejoice in God can enjoy laughing with him or at ourselves, but not at another at that person's expense.

Then there have come moments when the preacher simply must stop in a sermon because the throat is too tight and tears too close. I am embarrassed by those rare occasions and try not to allow my own emotions to shut down the entire communication process in preaching. But those moments, too, somehow fit in. In their own way they are a signal that the truth at hand is so powerful the preacher cannot move through it as one who is never brought to tears. Those moments need to be very, very rare. That intimate level of the preacher's humanity is best saved for the privacy of one's room or closest intimates.

I once heard a man describe his childhood memories of the preacher coming to tears in nearly every sermon. It became routine and a nuisance to good listening. No wonder the man looked back on his early days in church with recollections of uneasiness.

Do many who preach rewrite their sermons after as well as before preaching? This practice has become my own through an arrangement inherited from my predecessor. His sermons were transcribed, typed, printed and mailed out to a subscriber's list. When I followed him the practice continued. I have formed the habit of retyping Sunday sermons on Monday morning. It is not as onerous as one might imagine—in fact I often find that after outlining, writing, and twice preaching a sermon on Sunday, it is only on Monday morning at the rewriting that I am finally getting said what I think should be said. More important than a sermon mailing list is the value of writing and rewriting what is preached. The act of writing it down after the experiencing of preaching it is time well spent. It helps communication. It contributes something to what others find interesting enough to read. It also makes it possible for people to read a sermon long after the preaching of it from the pulpit.

▶*4*◀

The Preacher As Person Among People

My DECISION TO STUDY FOR THE PASTORAL MINISTRY came early in my seventeenth year. Among the solid factors that motivated me at the time were also some spurious ones as I look back on those days now. I recall being impressed by "the uniform." My father, who was in bread sales, wore a uniform. So did the milkman, postman, policeman, and airline pilot. Pastors, as I saw them as a boy in the Lutheran church, wore black or dark blue suits with ties of the same color. They always wore white shirts, and when functioning on Sundays wore black robes. I could not help noticing those things. Along with book-lined studies often redolent with cigar smoke (my brand of Lutherans allowed such), I began to associate certain sights and settings and smells with what it meant to be a preacher. These things were externals, of course, and had nothing to do with the substance of ministry. But they were externals that in their own way spoke to me of the pastor as a person. I thought that was good, although at the time my understanding of the set-apart ministry was little more than a millimeter deep. In spite of the superficiality of these externals, they helped me as a youth sense that somehow the preacher is a person set apart, but that this does not close off relationships with people. In fact, it helps to define them.

The nature of relationships between pastor and people is no small factor in what goes into preaching. The fruits of those relationships are rich for preaching. Dress, vestments, the study, and so on are of course surface matters and will vary widely. And the basic issue of pastor-people relationships is not altered by one of the most important facts concerning the pastoral ministry of more recent years: the calling of increasing numbers of women into the preaching office. Whether male or female, formally or casually dressed, equipped with a book-lined study or not even with a room for books, the heart of the relationships between preacher and hearers lies elsewhere.

God bestows an authority upon his Word. It is the authority that consoles and wins the contrite heart. Such an authority is the polar opposite of the supposed power that depends on image, charisma, or turn-around collars. The authority of the Word that offers Christ to people is rooted in the self-giving love and unmerited grace his cross proclaims. That is the authority which draws people freely to allegiance. Such an authority does not give me clout over others because I am called to witness the authoritative gospel. But it does set me apart; it holds me to my calling and sustains me in all the relationships that are mine with people. Being thus set apart happens without assuming airs of status as a member of the clergy. It means being set apart without throwing oneself at others on the strength of personality. Being set apart by Christ involves not losing people in the thick of full schedules, strictly held office hours, and constant reminders of what remains to meet the budget. People are set apart for God by his Spirit, through faith. The sign of that work of God is love for people. The relationships which grow out of that love are fundamental for the lifelong shaping of the person the preacher is.

The first circle of those relationships is pastor to family. Every pastor is, first of all, a son or daughter. Each of us comes with the stamp of our childhood and the lasting influence of home and upbringing. My blessing in this regard was to be born of parents who were of differing denominations until the later years of their lives. They nurtured me in such a way as to help me see from my earliest time that God has his people in more than one denominational fold.

My non-Lutheran mother was the most formative influence

in my spiritual growing up. No one gave me more support in my decision to go off to pre-seminary training. The first time I put on a black preaching gown in our living room her eyes filled with happy tears. She kept up a constant and enlightening correspondence with me all through my seminary training, responding with eagerness and insight into the theology I was learning and always helping me to keep people in view as my biblical, systematic, and historical theological course work went along.

My father, whose formal education had to be cut off at high school years because of farming duties on the Nebraska plains, drove with me to a small Kansas town and bore with me as I preached my first sermon. I can still recall his one-line summary as we drove out of the church yard: "Son, that was deep!" (a very open-ended comment). He took time off to come to the seminary campus and visit classes with me. My mother did the same in my college years. I received love, support, affirmation, critique, encouragement, and incentive to get on with the calling from those who brought me into the world. Later on, my older sister has opened up to me the beauty and richness of her own spiritual journey.

And of prime importance has been and continues to be my wife. There should be no stereotyping of the pastor's spouse. That person is best in the partnership role as he or she is fully and naturally at home in the faith and in caring relationship to the one who preaches. I find that encouragement and affirmation from many other sources truly count, but the word I wait for and the eye expression that means the most to me as the years go by is the voice and face of my wife. She loves me enough to let me know when there's egg on my face in the pulpit. She is interested enough in the pastoral calling to be ready to listen when I have things to talk about that are for no other ears.

My respect and esteem is boundless for preachers who have a sharply different marital or family situation. Knowing their courage and grace under personal burdens that are immense, I am humbled and honored to be their colleague in ministry. These are the men and women who personify the image of the pastor as the wounded healer. Their witness to Christ's grace as sufficient for their personal needs enables them to reach and minister to people whom others of us can never reach.

The gift given me and the congregation in the person of my wife is the gift of her being herself as a woman in Christ without pretense or role-playing. She prays with and for me, is happy to follow or lead with others in the congregation, keeps a lively household of children, foster children, parishioners, guests, foreign students, and occasional hungry street folk. We have our moments that we'd rather forget; we get tired and grumpy and wonder at times how college tuitions are going to be paid. But we're forgiven and forgiving and neither of us would rather be doing something else in some other place.

Children of clergy are also subject to stereotypes, but our four children seem happily free of daily wondering if they are fulfilling the requirements set by some parish board. One of the finest satisfactions in our parsonage is the fact that our children worship God because they love him and want to let it show. They have learned much as helpers in the household with the three dozen or so foster babies and children who have been with us over the years. They have understood that they need to work for their education and deliver in the classroom, since pastoral salaries are not notoriously excessive.

The children of the parsonage are, more often than they realize, a message about the ministry and minister himself. They are free in Christ to be about their lives in whatever direction he is pleased to lead them. They cherish daily the same forgiveness of sins that keeps their parents going. They are no small part of what I have learned and keep on learning about the joy and fulfillment of giving through serving.

Not at all frequently, but on certain occasions when the text and sermon situation seems altogether right, I have spoken of our marriage and our family in sermons. I have yet to have a parishioner let me know that it didn't fit. People long for reference to marriage and family life that flourishes in the midst of all the realities of our fallen nature. But one does not have to talk about it publicly very often. The life of the parsonage and the quality of relationships are there for most to see, and it is a sermon without words in its own right.

As future years bring increasing pressures upon marriage and family life in cultures all over the world, the incredibly abundant goodness of God I have been testifying to in our marriage and family life will have increasing importance.

I say these things with full respect for those men and women called to the single life. I recognize that their home and upbringing are equally vital, and their celibate calling by no means cuts off fulfilling and enriching relationships with those who are close to them. They, too, are a sign of the grace of Christ and have capacities for ministry not given to me. The point is that whether married or celibate, whether in parsonage family or in the collegiality of close-knit ties that flourish without a family, the one who preaches is profoundly affected by what occurs at this intimate level day after day.

The pastoral epistles rightly give prominence to this inner circle of the preacher's life. "The husband of one wife, temperate, sensible, dignified, hospitable, an apt teacher . . . he must manage his own household" well (1 Tim. 3:2–4) refers to gifts that are deep and lasting for ministry. Here is soil in which the seed of fulfilling relationships grows in such a way as to enrich the other, wider circles of life in which the pastor is a person among people.

I have spoken in the opening chapter of pastor-congregation relationships that flourish because of mutual love, respect, faith, shared experience, winsomeness, and a clear sense of spiritual purpose. I recall them now for the purpose of connecting each of those qualities to the set-apartness that authentic preaching reflects under the authority of the gospel. A seasoned teacher of preaching, Arndt Halvorson, has observed: "Novels derive their power from showing us people caught in, struggling with, destroyed by, or victorious over the issues which face us. In a novel we do not read *about* economics, politics, public and private morality, we meet people who are struggling with these pressures."[1]

I agree, but want to add how immediate and first-hand are the experiences which come daily to the preacher who lives with his eyes, ears, mind, and heart open to people who are not figures in a novel but living persons who are part of the network of life in which the preacher lives.

The authority of the Word punctures and exposes authoritarianism in us who preach. I know it from my experience with a parishioner who was among the first hospital patients I called on the first week after ordination. Shirley Krier was in the early stages of multiple sclerosis in 1954. She and I were within a month of each other in age; I could never remember who was older but she would regularly tell me that it was I who was the old one in case I forgot.

Her husband had found that marriage to a wife with this disease was hampering. He left her. In all the ensuing twenty-eight years of ministering to Shirley Krier in the hospitals, county homes, and nursing centers to which she was shuffled, I never met anyone in her family nor did she speak of their visiting her. As the disease gradually destroyed her muscle control, even to the point of her inability to focus her eyes, she found it ever harder to speak. The tongue just would not make the right moves for speech. But her soul and her sense of humor survived when virtually all else that made her human was wasted. If I would sometimes come to her bedside with Word and sacrament forgetting my own need to hear a clear word of truth about myself, her slowly spoken greeting did it. "Where'n the world have you been?" was her usual opening sentence, uttered with a terrific physical effort but also with a twinkle in her eye. She meant it. It is too long between visits, Pastor Lueking. Get better organized. Don't think you are the only one who can get over here to minister to me. Aren't there some others among the 1,800 members you can call upon? What kind of shepherd are you, anyway? All these sentiments underlay her colorful opening line. She was right in each of them. I had not shared the work of ministry well. My failure was in not equipping others to help in visiting the sick. Shirley was my best teacher in helping me see where I needed to grow.

And Shirley Krier never failed to say her thanks, to me and to others in the congregation who joined in ministry to her. At her burial there were fewer than six of us present on a blustery day in early spring, but I am in lifelong debt to this sterling Christian woman for outlasting despair, bitterness, loneliness, and the indescribable frustration that such a disease imposes.

Word authority spares the one who preaches the problem of trying to be too close with people at the expense of accepting the needed space that all humans require. Standing back at the right time and for the right reason is especially important for the Word to do its work. This is the opposite pitfall of authoritarian lording it over people. Yet it is no less a stumbling block. A misunderstanding lies at the heart of trying too hard, being too close. When it comes to the ultimate issues of life and death and our standing before God, Christians rightly expect the preacher to be much more than, and other than, nice. That backslapping kind of self-recommendation betrays a serious lack of confidence. It comes through underestimating the Word itself. Confidence and trust from people toward pastor flourishes in direct relation to the Word the preacher brings and the uncluttered witness the preacher makes to that Word.

People can find cronyism in many places. But the forced intimacy that phony camaraderie imparts obstructs rather than assists. It cannot help but make people wonder if this is a preacher or a huckster. Being a bearer of the awesome judgment and unfathomable mercies of God lays upon the preacher a requirement to let space remain so that the Word can be heard. I am not calling for aloofness but distance enough so that the listener can get perspective and hearing distance.

To apply the word dignity to that situation is more a testimony to the Word itself than a comment on a personality trait of the preacher. There really is an awesomeness to the human encounter with the living God. He isn't The Man Upstairs who invites unrepentant chumminess. He is the sovereign Creator, Redeemer, and Sanctifier of all. To come into his presence with a trembling heart is appropriate.

The messenger of such a numinous Presence needs to accept a certain distance that the Message creates. This fact, incidentally, does not limit itself to pastor-people connections. It also takes place in connection with any and every Christian who is serious about meeting God and relating to others in the light of that encounter.

Word authority makes the preacher other than one who

aspires to become the chief executive officer of a highly organized congregation, with flow-charts, elaborate committee-monitoring, and other evasions of the cure of souls. People may be grateful that a pastor administers well, but they want above all to know that the preacher prays with depth and knows the God of whom he speaks. Of course preachers share with others the responsibility of knowing how to read a financial report, but people long to hear from the pulpit the evidence of earnest and faithful wrestling with the mysteries of God in his ways with the world.

American congregational life is notoriously given to self-preoccupation. The machinery of congregational organization all too often drains off the major spiritual energies of believers who have rarely experienced the sense of being under Christ's lordship in mission to the world. Joseph Sittler's term, "the maceration of the minister," was an outcry against the enervating busyness of the preacher in all directions instead of immersion in and singular devotion to the Word-centeredness of ministry. That appeal still speaks to us.

My experience tells me that I become vulnerable to this threat of busyness because I let circumstances grow up around me that tempt me to try to do what others do better and should do. If I, the pastor, have to be the last word in every committee and board, if I am the harried money raiser, the one seeking and letting contracts, the one with the hard-hat on daily in the new building project, then I am neither preacher nor administrator. There aren't that many hours in the day nor are there that many energies placed in one body.

Word authority takes delight in equipping and sharing the wide range of gifts and duties that are part of congregation life. The preacher has one center of gravity, and that is the imparting of God's grace to sinners. Out of that center comes partnership with people in growing in joint ministry to the world. Let General Motors have its own realm; the preacher is not called to import that style into the assembly that gathers around Word and sacrament for inner nourishment and outward discipleship. The authority of the Word keeps the preacher on center and enables the preacher to keep housekeeping details in perspective and in other, more capable hands.

The pastor is a person, not only in the circle of family and the congregation, but also among colleagues. The support and influence of fellow clergy is a special resource for preaching and an important aspect of ministry with others.

It is noteworthy that Jesus never sent his disciples out alone, but two by two and more often in the larger company of his followers. Likewise, St. Paul did not journey to the Gentiles alone but always in the company of other apostles. There is something essentially collegial about the proclamation of the Christian gospel. Its servants are not prima donnas who function as solo voices. Servanthood in proclamation means that the preacher relates to fellow servants of the Word in such a way as to demonstrate in that collegiality the truth of the gospel coming through. Not only do preachers talk gospel; doing the truth must be the base for that speaking. The forgiveness we need for ourselves and proclaim to others has an authentic ring when people can see that forgiving relationships truly exist among those who preach and teach.

This is hard to see in the star-syndrome that not only can dominate media preachers but also does its damage in the jealousies, petty rivalries, and the general isolation from one another that can plague preachers anywhere. Conversely, the upbuilding of one another in the sharing of the practice, the mutual consolation and encouragement that comes through faithful conversation, the conscious labors of encouragement and example shown from pastor to pastor are clearly part of God's plan. These are important ways by which God provides maintenance for those he sets apart for ministry.

I began my ordained ministry under the wing of a senior pastor who cared greatly about this. Otto Geiseman was the kind of pastor among pastors who could be offended by the breakdown of collegiality through laziness, aimless ministry, and the sin of coasting through the pastorate without ever seeking growth. He once stood up in a pastoral conference, looked at his colleagues, and declared: "There's nothing wrong with us that reading one new book and getting our suits cleaned wouldn't help." This candor didn't win him elections to denominational office but that wasn't important. What did matter to him was joining with interested preachers in a group that would take on one worthwhile subject of ministry a month, prepare for it, read up on it, reflect upon their own ministries in the light of it, and share the results in learning sessions that were a gift to all.

In the late 1960s I became one among many pastors, ministers, and priests in the United States who has benefited from the leaven of the Academy of Parish Clergy. It continues as a group of men and women in congregation-based ministry who accept the discipline of growing and helping others grow through continuing education, colleague groups, regional and annual convocations, and a journal of our experiences.

Preachers influence one another. I received my earliest impressions about preachers from the gentle, faithful man who was my pastor from age four through my late teens. To this day I benefit from reading other sermons and I love to hear other men and women preach. I am instructed by the fresh ways of doing ministry and preaching that come to me through contacts with others in ministry across the denominational spectrum.

I am writing these chapters in the midst of a sabbatical visit in western Kenya where each afternoon takes me to lay or clergy Christians in nearby congregations. From them I am getting a picture of how and why the Christian faith is growing faster in Africa than anywhere else in the world. I look forward to the continuance of this sabbatical journey of four months from Europe through Africa to India, China, and Japan—all in the interest of contact, conversation, sharing my ministry and learning from other clergy and lay persons about preaching and congregational life in the world today.

The congregation I serve has graciously commended me to this splendid opportunity. They released me for four months of my service to them, knowing that I shall return that much deeper and broader as a person for continuing ministry there. This is an unusual example of something that can take place in other than global traveling to congregations. Wherever and whenever congregations encourage their clergy to rub elbows with other preachers and see what is on the other side of the hill, it never means hindrance but always gain for congregation, preacher and all. Begrudging those contacts is short-circuiting everyone.

Preachers need to help congregations see this and challenge

the people to grow along with the one who preaches. In certain things that have to do with the art and craft of preaching, fellow practitioners are the best and principal teachers and evaluators of the preaching ministry. We are persons among fellow preachers, and the impact of this positive relationship has a direct contribution to the substance and form of preaching.

Our personhood, grounded in the authority of the Word we proclaim, is always relational. We who preach are ministered to in family, in congregation, in collegial ties, and by people beyond the congregation. We perform ministry and proclaim Christ in these concentric circles which comprise our days. In each of them something essential is given us, and we in turn have our opportunity to give back what we receive. Behind each sermon the web of these essential relationships always stands. The preacher is ever a debtor. He is a person among people; she is one who can always recognize the "we" and "us" in the blessed ties with people who nourish and sustain us for preaching.

▸5◂

The Guidelines

ONE WOULD LIKE TO ASSUME THAT THE NEED to appropriately integrate people into preaching would be self-evident and that everyone would come by it naturally. It doesn't turn out this way, of course. Incorporating people into preaching is a learned art. My own experiences, both successful and calamitous, are offered here as a beginning point from which the reader may well add more.

A cardinal rule is discretion. This often poses a dilemma. The one who preaches is allowed entrance into some vital experience in another's life and wants very much to let the impact of that significant event have a much wider scope of influence. But the first requirement is a responsible decision as to whether this person and moment can be shared appropriately or whether by its very nature it must forever remain a matter among the person, God, and the pastor who has been permitted to know of it. Unquestionably there are such experiences. Most often they come to the preacher's attention through the confession-absolution function of the ministry.

Quite obviously when an individual entrusts some personal experience of transgression to the minister or priest, that act of fidelity is never to be broken. The name, the other persons involved, the particulars of the circumstance deserve the strictest confidence and any misuse of such a sacred bond puts an end to a relationship that is important for our spiritual health. That is not only pertinent to the bond between pastor and person; it applies to the general relationship between pastor and congregation.

If people hear some distressing sin of another paraded before the membership in anything so public as a sermon, or are even given grounds to start guessing, no one will ever be foolish enough to take his own personal struggles to such a betrayer.

Is there a way in which discretion and fidelity can work together so as to preserve the confidentiality of the individual and at the same time let the power and beauty of a contrite heart find expression? I believe there is. My basis for this is that in three decades of preaching in the same congregation I have yet to hear a complaint of a confidence betrayed. Several particulars of discretion go into it.

The first is *time*. Something that has taken place quite recently and may well be painfully vivid in the mind of the one who went through that personal hell must be kept in silence. But then ten years may pass, or longer. The individual involved has moved away or died. The membership of the congregation has changed as it inevitably does. People who may have been adversely affected by the situation are no longer in hearing distance. Or the preacher may have moved to another congregation and thus the setting is entirely cut off from that former person and place.

Can such things legitimize sharing some lesson of life that another's learning the hard way teaches? I have done so and have added such safeguards to confidentiality as telling the story with no reference to whether it was a man or woman— simply referring to the person as another Christian. I have omitted any reference to an identifying setting so that the instructiveness of the experience can come through without damaging the integrity of the pastoral relationship or throwing discretion to the winds.

I am willing to risk being regarded as a contriver or a shrinker of an earlier experience that still stays with me. Sometimes, I find, the urge to let a powerful experience bring blessing to a wider audience prevails; I'm glad to stand by it.

Another basic guideline is consistency with the main textual point. The experiences of people may be misused as a substitute for sound textual work. When that is the problem then the reference to people in preaching is a distraction rather than a support to the central theme of the sermon. "This great insight of the Bible reminds me of a story" is a more perilous sentence from the pulpit than most of us realize. The crucial purpose is that the hearer's mind gets to the goal of realizing: "I see the truth of God more clearly now." If the outcome of the illustration is "What a funny story" or "I wonder if the person referred to might be . . . ?" then the point has been lost and the illustration has backfired. But consistency between the text and the experience greatly enhances the function of preaching, especially when the experience is of the sort that can lead the hearer to be a part of the textual truth and find ready handles of application to his or her own life.

For example, Jesus called for persistence in prayer in the Parable of the Importunate Woman (Luke 18:1–8). My mind turns to a father who continued in persevering prayer for years for a daughter who walked out on her husband and children for another man. I knew of his long train ride to another city in the dead of winter, his knocking at his daughter's door only to have her close it in his face. I was at his burial and knew of his intercession for this daughter among the last words he could utter. And I knew of this daughter's slow but ultimate coming to herself, well after her father's death, and her penitent turning to the Father above with deep regret for the time and affection lost by her wrong decisions at an earlier time.

The stamina and drama of faith embedded in that parable of Jesus was no doubt drawn from life as he saw it in a widow of his time. Its connection to life was abundantly clear in the faithfulness of one who prayed and kept on praying, but did not live to see the prayers answered. He died in the hope that God would yet bring an answer in his own time and way.

Again, the apostle Paul announces that we contend not just with humans who are intractable in evil, but that we are arrayed against whole systems and institutionalized evil that bring woe onto whole nations and civilizations (Eph. 6:12). Human experience consistent with such a text takes the form of protest against national priorities which exalt guns over butter and vested interests which exalt profits over the plight of people whose children starve because of the pittance their fathers receive in order that others may live in luxury.

The formidable, pervasive obduracy of sin which is the point of the Ephesians text also comes home to me and finds its way into preaching through my experience of being completely deceived by a family that came at Christmas time seeking help in housing. The five-month aftermath of having to finally evict the people from a church member's home (which they nearly wrecked without ever intending to pay a penny's rent) was a learning experience in the text that put gray hair on my head.

The Psalm writer speaks of the joy of coming together with others for the worship of God (Ps. 100), and some stranger is kind enough to write a brief note on what it meant for him to be at worship with us for several weeks while he was in our city for a brief training course in his business. He helped us see what the text proclaims; his letter was its own kind of consistent comment on the text and fit well into the preaching of it.

Living day in and day out under the Word and in ministry to people cannot help but offer the welcome evidences of all kinds of biblical truth taking root and making a difference in the lives of people. One need not strain to exaggerate or distract or titillate or entertain or stoop to gossip. The powerful, instructive life experiences of people are there in abundance. Consistency with the text is required in their selection and use.

The issue of propriety belongs in this list of guidelines. One of the things which must distinguish preaching from the contemporary penchant for shock techniques to numb the senses and flatten out the humanity of people is the decision to keep preaching within the boundaries of propriety. This is particularly true in reference, both in affirmation and in judgment, to matters of ethical behavior. The novelist Alan Paton did not have to titillate his readers with prurient detail in describing the moment when a married white man gave in to his sexual passion for a black woman. He handled that moment in one sentence: "And there, God forgive, he possessed her."[1]

Sexual references in preaching need not be excessive or clinical. All of us know physiology. What needs attention, diagnosis, and remedy is the spiritual root of the matter, as our Lord himself teaches us in the Sermon on the Mount.

On the other side of the problem, Victorian embarrassment to even speak clearly about this aspect of our lives is not propriety. Forty-five years ago, as a boy of ten, I heard a preacher refer to a disease "that because of the dignity of the pulpit I will not mention." I spent the rest of the sermon time wondering what that ailment was, and never found out until asking my father later. Syphilis is not a scatological term and it would not have assaulted the dignity of the pulpit if the preacher had been clear in speaking of the problem. His effort at propriety was a distraction.

Where the fine line of propriety is drawn is a matter of sanctified common sense, and propriety will be differently defined in different cultures. A sermon I heard recently in Kenya dealt directly with circumcision practices which play such a large role in this culture. No one was shocked or regarded the preacher's word as fully lacking in propriety.

In an American pulpit the same subject might be inappropriate because circumcision has no such corresponding place as a rite of passage. The dependable rule I have found is this: What I cannot speak of candidly and clearly out of my biblical faith doesn't get into the public proclamation; what I can, does.

Thus, years ago, the time when a gifted young man came into my study, sat down, put his head in his hands, and let out a torrent of tears in telling me that he was a homosexual ultimately became a part of a sermon several years later. This was so because of his permission and his help to me in beginning to understand the tortuous existence of a fellow human being who has tried the route of bar-cruising, compulsive sexual encounters, and the wrongness of both hiding it and flaunting it. It was indeed right to express in preaching the testimony of that Christian man and the instructiveness of his holding fast to grace in seeking wholeness under Christ and the way of righteousness amidst the complexities of his situation. The dignity, clarity, and sensitivity in speaking of such matters is a paradigm for how we get out of the closets of our own ignorance and bias and begin to move toward healing and mutual upbuilding in difficult situations of our discipleship. Not just that it is spoken of in sermons, but the propriety of that speaking is essential.

One learns to touch substance and avoid trivializing a text when speaking of what people live through but usually it is via the hard way. I didn't mean to be trivial when once referring to a lightweight incident in my life, but did so in introducing a text that was anything but lightweight (Rom. 7:15–25), in which Paul wrestles with the enigma of being both saint and sinner. A woman was present in the congregation who was wanting help at a far deeper level than my rather glib anecdotal introductory comment. I put an obstacle in her way. She helped me see that in a brief note which arrived on Monday morning. Ever after, as I see her in church, I am reminded of the help she gave me in sparing the people trivia. Preaching is too momentous an event to reduce to glibness or chatty cuteness.

The opposite of trivia is substance. It doesn't have to be heavy-handedness, grim seriousness, or always referring to people who are in crisis, illness, or death. Substance can be drawn out of the everydayness of our lives, which makes up so much of our waking hours. Doesn't it count that a person of faith accepts the routineness of the flatlands of our existence without constantly looking for a sign or wondering if there is any life in the soul? Hearers need to know that this is a given of the Christian vocation, and that there are spaces in life when little that is exciting seems to be happening.

The fact of persevering through such ordinariness of life is not trivial. It happens because of the substance of faith, which does not depend upon constant heights but plods through the long valleys with contentment that the gospel of Christ's grace is bread for that part of the journey, too.

People need help in marriage, raising the family, finding meaning in work, and accepting the new circumstances that new stages of life bring. Help can and does come in sermon references to people who learn how to forbear one another in love through decades of marriage.

Honoring the experience of older members and citing their long-term faithfulness in living through the years has strong biblical warrant and is another way of weaving into preaching the stories of people. They may not look spectacular but they have stayed at their calling instead of gradually slipping away into spiritual oblivion.

Raising children and releasing them to their own directions of life happens all along with a quiet sort of heroism; lifting it up for appreciation in preaching helps to rescue it from being taken for granted.

Among the best ways I have found to do this is not only to talk about such "ordinary" people who yet have extraordinary substance, but to plan with them their own personal participation in preaching from time to time. Where possible I have asked a couple who are working at teaching prayer and discipleship to their children to step to the lectern and take some sermon time to tell their story of parenting in the light of Christ's lordship. Men and women who daily experience the meaning of Christian vocation in their job setting also help in preaching as they speak their witness.

Varied aspects of the Christian journey are illumined this way, not because the individual experiences have to be spectacular but because the people who persevere in the faith are notable witnesses who help us see the faithfulness of God in unpretentious circumstances. Such a method is not an every-Sunday occurrence; otherwise it loses its edge. But including a variety of people in a variety of life circumstances helps avoid the pitfalls of sameness in sermon references and the neglecting of the less spectacular sides of the whole picture of following Christ in faith.

When testimony is made to those who experience personally the realities which are beyond the preacher's own experience, hearers are less likely to get sidetracked into private mental arguments with the preacher as to whether he knows anything about this side of life.

Some splendid moments of effective preaching have come to us in our congregation through an older, single woman who spoke of her years of employment followed now by new opportunities of volunteering time and service in a community agency for aged and shut-in people needing nutritious meals.

Another man in a position of corporate leadership helped dispel the Scrooge image of the boss by witness to the sustaining goodness of God in his care for employees in an increasingly tight job market.

We've heard witness from collegians home for vacation

time, from children who often can see the ways of Providence
in things we adults take for granted, and from refugees who
by their very presence in the assembly remind us of the gift
of freedom in worship and opportunity in service.

The methods will vary, but the rule remains the same—substance and not trivia as the preacher keeps a sharp eye for
what lies just under the surface of the most ordinary looking
life. These lives preach more effectively than highly publicized
people who make guest appearances on some religious television programs. Grace, not hype, makes them effective.

People references need to proclaim gospel, not simply talk
about life. The Good News is not any kind of religious talk
or casual reference to this or that in the Bible. The apostolic
gospel is that God gave his Son over to death for our sins
and in raising Jesus Christ from the dead has established his
lordship as the one sure thing that holds good for all people
till the end of the ages. Both preacher and whomever the
preacher occasionally engages for personal witness in preaching need to keep that truth uppermost. It is never to be taken
for granted that this gospel is clearly seen as the heart of
witness. In preparing people for membership in the congregation I have often used a simple four-statement format, asking
them to make note of whether and when they hear the gospel
as the four are read off:

Do unto others as you would have them do unto you.

God helps those who help themselves.

Christ Jesus died for our sins and was raised again.

Keeping the Ten Commandments is the heart of our faith.

Learning the responses to that exercise always teaches me
how constant is the task of keeping the biblical gospel uppermost in preaching. Christ's cross and resurrection for us is
the one lifeline that holds us to God and equips us for functioning faithfully in his world. The Golden Rule, the responsibility to use our talents, the continued response to the law
of God which convicts our conscience of sin, all have their
place. But none is the gospel. All stand in relation to the

gospel and all have their place in the experiences of people. Citing people in preaching needs to be constantly focused upon the redeeming work of God in Jesus Christ as the heart of faith that makes everything else fit and work toward the end of the praise of God and partnership with him in his mission in the world.

How can the preacher make use of personal experience? In an essential sense, all authentic preaching is an expression of the Spirit who has laid hold on the preacher's heart. That does not mean the preacher establishes every truth of God by her own knowledge, assent, and trust, nor does it mean that the preacher is talking of nothing other than his own life experiences under the gospel. But all preaching, to be preaching, is witness. It is imperfect witness, to be sure, constricted by the limits of the person who is preaching. But it is witness to God's grace nonetheless. Preachers who have lost the faith once held need help in being restored to it; in that time the one so afflicted should step aside from preaching until a clear, persuasive note can be sounded again.

It is well to say so if a text has a greatness far beyond the preacher's own grasp. The incredible scenario of trust in the face of impending execution that St. Paul lays out in Philippians 1 is well beyond the circle of experience of most of us. Joseph Sittler once recalled that he opened a sermon on that passage with a candid acknowledgment: "This text refers to something I do not know by experience." That did not make him silent about the great truth to be preached. It was an honest word about the text as surpassingly greater than the preacher's part in it. That is both a positive expression of humility as well as an accurate sizing up of the actual situation. In that regard preacher and hearer are in the same boat.

But when the power of the text has entered with transforming vitality into the preacher's own experience, it must be shared. Sometimes that is best done in less than a dozen words: "I know this truth from my own experience. . . ." On another occasion the preacher may share an episode of life that cannot be capsuled in a dozen words. Lengthier personal reference needs disciplined attention. Because no single one of us can live at fever pitch all the time, personal reference is appropriately sparing. Yes, the preaching act itself is witness to the preacher's affirmation of faith. But it hardly means that the congregation should be peppered by ceaseless anecdotes out of the preacher's life.

The same rubric holds true for illustrative preaching in general. A sound work of pulpit witness may have at most one or two extended references to the biblical text illumined by what has occurred in the lives of believers. People cannot benefit from examples that begin to multiply beyond the ability of the mind to digest and assimilate, and people do not need excessive illustrations to get the point. Economy of reference in favor of quality of substance is the rule.

One final note of emphatic importance: in incorporating humor or irony into preaching to help buttress the textual point, it is mandatory that the butt of any such humor be the preacher and not some other. The risk of humor that is at another's expense is the risk of sarcasm. People can perform the necessary transfer from preacher to self when it comes to the humor of our fallibility. When humor is part of the joy and victory of Christlike living, let everyone share the fun! But when the subject is the distance yet to travel to that goal and the ludicrousness of our bypaths along the way, let the instructive laughter be at the preacher's own expense. As Christ's fools, what do we have to hide—or to lose?

▶ 6 ◀

People in the Daily Work of Ministry

THE PARABLES OF JESUS ARE DRAWN FROM LIFE situations, as every interpreter keeps on telling us. But the point deserves continued emphasis. A man went out to sow seed, a woman scoured her household looking for a lost coin, a man fell among robbers en route to Jericho, a woman kept on pestering a judge for a hearing; such settings of life experiences reflect Jesus' keen eye to see the ordinary as the surrounding situation in which truth is to be told.

The daily work of ministry is an endless source of such settings for all of us who minister in Christ's name to people. If it is one's custom to begin the day with prayer, a petition that belongs as the day starts out is for eyes to see and ears to hear the significance of people in the course of the daily work. Michel Quoist's *Prayers* is a model of faithful hearing and seeing of the meaning of people and commonplace things as the workshop of the Spirit. He sees the glint of meaning for ministry in a chalkboard, a swing, a tractor, a twenty-dollar bill, a bald head, or a night football game. Listen to his perceptive sense for people as he remembers before God the people and the situations of a day in his life:

> Thank you, Lord, thank you.
> Thank you for all the gifts that you have given me today,
> Thank you for all I have seen, heard, received.

Thank you for the water that woke me up, the soap that smells
good, the toothpaste that refreshes.

Thank you for the clothes that protect me, for their color and
their cut.

Thank you for the newspaper so faithfully there, for the comics
(my morning smile), for the report of useful meetings, for
justice done and for big games won.

Thank you for the street-cleaning truck and the men who
run it, for their morning shouts and all the early noises.

Thank you for my work, my tools, my efforts.

Thank you for the metal in my hands, for the whine of the
steel biting into it, for the satisfied look of the supervisor
and the load of finished pieces.

Thank you for Jim who lent me his file, for Danny who gave
me a cigarette, for Charlie who held the door for me.

Thank you for the welcoming street that led me there, for
the shop windows, for the cars, for the passers-by, for all
the life that flowed swiftly between the windowed walls
of the houses.

Thank you for the boy I watched playing on the sidewalk
opposite,

Thank you for his roller-skates and for his comical face when
he fell.

Thank you for the morning greetings I received, and for all
the smiles.

Thank you for the mother who welcomes me at home, for
her tactful affection, for her silent presence.

Thank you for the roof that shelters me, for the lamp that
lights me, for the radio that plays, for the news, for music
and singing.

Thank you for the bunch of flowers, so pretty on my table.

Thank you for being there, Lord.

Thank you for listening to me, for taking me seriously, for
gathering my gifts in your hands to offer them to your Father.

Thank you, Lord,

Thank you.[1]

Such a gift of perceptive seeing is ever welcome and belongs
among the things we do well to pray for.

We have virtually taken into our language a German word
that marks out one of the places in daily ministry where the
significance of people is found. The term *Seelsorge*—the care

and cure of souls—defines the whole attitude of wanting to see, wanting to hear, wanting to bring healing to people's whole needs in the light of Christ's grace. It is a term that needs recovering, particularly in our time when the language, tools, and assumptions of psychology and psychiatry have been sought by too many clergy at the expense of the *Seel* (soul) content of the *Sorge* process.

Ministry to people in the realities of their daily life situations begins, proceeds, and works toward the goal of the spiritual center of human life reconnected, healed, and strengthened in the mystery and kindness of God's heart. *Seelsorge* empowers people because of the primacy of the fruits of the Spirit rather than personality theories derived solely from the psychiatric disciplines. *Seelsorge* may mean teamwork between clergy and those who are skilled in those disciplines, which indeed offer medical help that people may need. And those who are carers of the soul may find their ministry aided by the acquiring of some of those skills. But something vital is lost if they forget the soul and neglect the renewing power of repentance and faith. The call to minister as a bearer of the Word is distinctive; it is at the heart of *Seelsorge.*

Hospitals are places clergy get to know quickly. Whether it be a two-room clinic or a sprawling medical center complex of hundreds of rooms and millions of dollars of sophisticated medical equipment, people are there and ministry to people in that time and place of life has a particular promise—together with some perils, too.

The first thing that most of us need to get over is a sense of being cowed by the sheer fact of the hospital and those who function in it. Granger Westberg, a theologian at home in the medical world, has often spoken of the modern heresy that healing can't go on apart from stainless steel. Up and down the halls are important-looking people dressed in the various uniforms of the medical hierarchy. People on the hospital staff, from charwoman all across the spectrum to the heart-transplant surgeon have tangible things to do and tangible things with which to work. The pastor comes with the things that are unseen, which St. Paul claims are not therefore transient but eternal. People come to regard the hospital as the modern temple where the wonders of science are held to be the ultimate efficacy, because they do not see that their deepest needs and solutions lie in their souls.

In hospitals the threatening forces that inveigh against soul and body and mind are less hidden. If the situation is such that one must leave the familiar setting of home and daily routines and go to a hospital, a stirring takes place at the deeper levels of our interior life. It may be no bigger than a raindrop on the far horizon of an inner uneasiness, but a rivulet of anxiety is let loose nonetheless. An occasion for *Seelsorge* is at hand.

People who have been hospitalized over thirty-five times tell me that those inner forebodings never disappear. In varying degrees of awareness, everyone becomes more mindful of the truth that life ends, death threatens, existence is bounded, as hospital time comes around.

I once saw that fear take over a grown man so strongly that as I walked into the hospital room to minister to him he was walking out. He had received word of a major tumor problem within the half hour; as soon as the doctor explained the matter to him (with great empathy and care for the patient's anxiety, his roommate told me) and left the room, the man got up, dressed, and walked out of the hospital and did not return. It's a one-time experience in my three decades of hospital calling, but the memory of it and the instructiveness of it stay with me.

Hospitals are places where clergy are called upon to get to the point. Early in my ordained ministry I entered a hospital room and began talking in a way that the patient perceived to be circuitous and wordy. She cut me off in mid-sentence of some pleasantry with this: "What I need is for you to get down on your knees at my bedside and *in one short sentence of prayer* beg God to get me through this half hour." I did. He did. And she did.

When I am called to an emergency room at 2 A.M. and stand next to a person who can only talk with his eyes because everything else is occupied with life-sustaining machinery, the whole range of faith, theology, training, belief, experience, is at stake. Then, above all, it becomes clear that the house of life built upon the rock of divine grace doesn't cave in when the winds are howling and terror threatens. Then, a grasped hand, a steady look into an eye that is pleading, a firm word of Scripture—these are the most irreplaceable medicines for the inner needs of life that the person can receive.

If the minister has no transcendent Word, no witness to life over death, no testimony to divine grace over the chaos of disease, the emergency room is emptier than ever. The minister is there to minister God's grace and promise. That witness is vital, and when that gospel is truly the Good News in the midst of an otherwise lethal situation, the emergency room is where God draws near to do what he alone can do—overrule fear and move the anxious heart to hold fast to his promise.

It isn't always the extremity of the emergency room that sets the stage for *Seelsorge*. I learned anew the meaning of ministry and the significance of people as recipients of grace from a friend whose wife was battling a major disease. After months of daily struggle with cancer, this husband sat down and wrote his wife a letter. She was at home at this stage of her illness, but he nevertheless put this thought down in writing for her benefit.

What is the worst thing, the absolute worst thing, that can happen to us? He then listed things that would indeed be a devastation in their lives: the loss of their house through fire, the brutalizing of her body by a rapist, the atrophying of affection and loyalty of their children, the removal of one or the other's eyesight through an accident or the loss of their health and life itself through disease. He told her: "None of these is the worst thing that can happen to us. The worst thing to befall us is that we would be separated from the love of God. That worst thing shall not happen to us."

Then he quoted the passage from Romans 8 that had become their rainbow overarching the darkness of this hard time in their lives:

> Who shall separate us from the love of Christ? Shall tribulation, or distress, or persecution, or famine, or nakedness, or peril, or sword? . . . No, in all these things we are more than conquerors through him who loved us. For I am sure that neither death, nor life, nor angels, nor principalities, nor things present, nor things to come, nor powers, nor height, nor depth, nor anything else in all creation will be able to separate us from the love of God in Christ Jesus our Lord (Rom. 8:35–39).

That is the point. This friend, whose gifts of mind and spirit are extraordinary, kept the core of *Seelsorge* uppermost through the long months of an inch-by-inch battle with her disease. In the final hour of her life, his ministry to his wife took the form of these simple words as he held her hand and stroked her forehead ever so gently: "You love Jesus; Jesus loves you."

In so many moments since, I have repeated that question to people made anxious by the onset of disease: What is the worst thing that can happen to you and me? . . . But that worst thing cannot happen to us, now that Christ has suffered that worst thing at Golgotha for our sake and is risen and present at our side through every shadowy valley.

When the ultimate Enemy is known to have been already defeated, the penultimate situations of hospital ministry can be freed up for courage, humor and other graces. A woman told me, long after a hospital call, "I'm grateful your visit was short; I was on the bedpan the whole time." Children have a wonderful way of keeping touch with their outside interests when confined to a hospital. I recall a nine-year-old opening one eye before prayer to ask: "Who are the Cubs playing today?" In that foggy world of post-operative recovery a handsome woman woozily lamented with a brave grin: "Here you are and my hair is a mess. . . ."

Hospital visits also reveal the stubbornness of our resistance to the bedrock truth of our right-standing with God, that it is all by grace and not works. A man who has been a church member for sixty years or more told me, after my rejoicing with him in the recovery he was experiencing: "Yes, I guess I've been a pretty good boy, haven't I?" Again we go back to square one, the unearned gift of grace that underlies all our recoveries.

We know people and are known by people in new ways when traveling together through the stress of disease. The bonding that takes place between pastor and people is a sign of the mutuality of ministry. I am blessed in the witness of courage and trust in God that people display.

That is the main thing I had to share with a parishioner who has trouble with ordained people in general, and especially when he was the patient in a hospital visited by a preacher who got busy with Scripture and prayer before asking for that privilege. The brittleness of that parishioner's telling me that I can come thereafter when he asks for a pastor instead of a lay bringer of the Word is one more time I have learned from people.

The preacher really does have to respect the person when illness makes that person miserable and vulnerable. All manner of previous hurts and slights and frustrations can surface and need to be understood and put aside if ministry is to be welcomed. The preacher needs to be prepared to walk out of the room and let another do the ministering work at times. It is not common, but when it does happen there is no gain in being upset. Let another minister. The main thing is that ministry goes on.

Mercifully, the book of Acts does not record many church meetings and the earliest congregations seem to have done remarkably well without them. But meetings are part of all congregational existence. They are among the most underestimated occasions for recognizing the ministry of people and carrying out the same to people. Congregations are voluntary organizations. People come and serve because they are willing. Time and energy and the investment of individual talents that are part of every meeting, large or small, reveal no small miracle each time they occur. That is easy to forget, particularly when meetings are routine and must cover tedious ground.

But preachers need to remember what a group of lay people helped me recognize years ago when we worked through a series on the meaning of Christian faith and daily work. This is the point: a congregation is one of the few places where many men and women are not under the constant pressure of having to measure up but in the circle of grace. In so much of the daily work situation, people are measured by their productivity, by their contribution to the sales record and the profit sheet, by their agility in out-maneuvering those who are angling for their position or by their staying ahead of the competition. They are perpetually under those accusatory questions: Did you produce enough? Are you staying ahead? What more can be gained from you? What more can you get from others? A congregation is a different place when that gathering is mindful of its charter in the grace of God. People find acceptance because of who they are, not what they do. People can fail without being fired. The great thing is not to beat out the other one, but to lay one's talents and experience alongside the other's for the greater good. So often it is in meetings that this graceful spirit is a reality among the practical doings and decisions of parish life. People who have been wounded by the relentless competitiveness of the workplace have found healing and much needed affirmation when sitting in a circle of approving eyes.

It isn't always that the daily job is the destroyer and the congregation is the restorer. We all know that the situation can be reversed. People can and do find integrity and God-given cooperativeness in their relationships at work, only to be disillusioned by pettiness and backbiting in the congregation.

I have in my memory a permanent slot for a brief note sent to me some twenty-five years ago: "The only time you have paid any attention to me is the one time you wrote me asking why my offerings were so little. Maybe there was one other time—a seconds-long greeting at the church door when you addressed me by the wrong name. . . ." Short notes like that deserve remembering.

That person was right, and had the grace to receive my penitence and desire for amendment of pastoral life. Every person counts; there is no such thing as deadwood on the parish roster. People are there who are hurting, or who are careless about the gathered life of God's people perhaps, but who are people nonetheless. How we think and talk of them reveals much about our own spiritual maturity or lack of it.

Collisions of will and divergence of viewpoint occur in church meetings. These must enhance rather than bring retreat from ministry to and by people. Conflict situations are inevitable in congregational life. The temptation to avoid them is strong, especially when the pastoral leader is directly involved as a result of being faithful to the calling. Such leadership, of course, is challenged. And when in public meetings people of an opposite view air their consternation with pastoral leadership one comes face to face with one of the most sensitive and demanding moments of ministry.

The task is to keep one's own defensive instincts at bay, to accept the persons doing the vehement speaking without accepting the judgments they offer, to answer them calmly and respectfully in order to inject into the tense atmosphere some essentials necessary for communication as Christians.

People who disagree are still fellow members of the Body of Christ. Church meetings are settings to let that show. What unites us is greater than what divides us. It does happen that people come to the point of leaving for another church home. Releasing them without condemnation or self-justifying squabbles is difficult but necessary.

When a parish conflict situation is major and long-lasting it must not overshadow everything all the time. With my wife and closest friends I have learned the blessing of the four-minute rule. At home or on social occasions, we keep an eye on the watch and after a maximum of four minutes' talk about the latest episode in the lengthy struggle, the subject is dropped. Giving controversy unlimited time and energy leads to an obsession with these things and the illusion that this matter in the congregation is the main event in the church and world of our time.

I have already written about the decisive importance of trust and confidentiality in the confession-absolution moments between pastor and people. The point has importance here as it connects congregational life with preaching. I have found times in the midst of such ministry, or at the conclusion of a session in which a Christian has been utterly honest with God in my presence and received his pardoning Word, I have asked the person if I am permitted to use this experience for the good of some other without breaking the seal of confidentiality. When that permission is granted—and usually it is—the victory of divine grace travels on in a wider swath.

When that permission is not given or when the person has trouble thinking about any possible use of it that does not imply revealing who has been involved, the matter stops there and the person is assured. The first and second letters of Paul to the Corinthians are richly instructive on the matter of everybody learning the way of grace in a congregation of no half-hearted sinners. One of the satisfying and hopeful things that people can count on as they look back on the debris of faithless living is the fact that others can be spared such a painful road. In this, too, God is able to work for good.

The daily rounds of ministry take the preacher outside as well as inside the congregation. As Augustine observed centuries ago, God has some of his people outside the church just as Satan has some of his people inside the church. As tempting as it is to draw up a list of Who's Who, the temptation must be withstood. One meets men and women who, even though they do not know it, are useful in God's providential work for the world. They are to be found in all walks of life, and when it comes to preaching, these people have a part. If we Christians can take our place in the world as witnesses rather than judges, we remain well positioned to relate to people of all kinds with interest in them for their own sake and with an eye toward how it is that their lives are part of the larger pattern of God's work in our world.

Every day in ministry is a living laboratory, and each person encountered in the daily course of work is a textbook.

◆7◆

The Wide Range of Human Experiences

PREACHING THAT MIRRORS FAITH AT WORK IN PEOPLE presents a broad spectrum of life experiences. Throughout this book so far the varied landscape of people living the faith in the congregation and in the world has been here and there evident. It is useful now to look at the roles of people in a more coherent way. Every one who preaches will have a unique way of listing these experiences, but here are basics which turn up in some manner or another in every congregation.

Sin and temptation.   The core of the biblical doctrine of sin and the resulting condition of fallen humanity is in Pogo's famous one-liner: "We have met the enemy and he is us." Our problem, before God, in relation to others, and with ourselves, is sin. In our Lord's Parable of the Prodigal Son, sin is shown as a condition, not merely an act. The headstrong boy leaves home, breaks a relationship, turns life inward upon himself in the far country, and then lives with the swine.

As long as the believer lives, there is the Archdeceiver with whom to contend, both in personal temptation as well as participation in political, social, economic, and ideological systems that crush people and defy God. With good reason, then, many services of worship begin not with congratulating each other on being so superior to all the sleepyheads that never get to church, but with these words or others similar in meaning:

Most merciful God, we confess that we are in bondage to
sin and cannot free ourselves. We have sinned against you
in thought, word, and deed, by what we have done and what
we have left undone. We have not loved you with our whole
heart; we have not loved our neighbors as ourselves. For the
sake of your Son, Jesus Christ, have mercy on us. Forgive us,
renew us, and lead us, so that we may delight in your will
and walk in your ways, to the glory of your holy name.

To say Amen after repeating those words or other forms
of corporate confession is to take part in a major revolution
week after week. Though baptized and made God's children
by his grace in Christ, every child of his still has a lifelong
battle with the subtle pockets of resistance to his lordship.
The hardest task in preaching is to set forth the law of God
to people in such a way that hearers say: "There's my problem.
That's where I'm missing the mark," and then move on to
the remedy which is the gospel.

When the law and its power to expose sin are absent or
muted, the gospel is the answer to the question that the hearer
has not yet asked. St. Paul, having felt the full weight of
the law, asked with passionate intensity: "Wretched man that
I am, who will deliver me from this body of death?"

That moment of truth can come with jarring force. A husband who battered his wife cannot lift his head to look another
in the eye, so deep is his shame for pummeling the woman
he married. A busy and successful surgeon is confronted head-
on by a long-standing patient's widow who was told by
the doctor when she phoned to tell him she thought her husband was dead: "Wait an hour and if he's cold, call this
number. . . ."

A man who has bedded down scores of other women finally
comes face to face with his emptiness and the boredom of
random copulation. A woman who has done the same with
successive male partners feels like a worthless whore (her own
words) when she sees a mother cheering up her sick child
in the hospital, where this distressed woman drove alone to
have her second abortion. A teenage boy, whose estranged
father has left the family for another man, talks to the son
once or twice a year by phone and berates him with scathing
sarcasm, steals a gun and walks toward a vacant lot to put

a bullet through his brain. I happened to meet him and gave him a lift in the back seat of my car, where he accidentally fired the bullet intended for his head—or mine—through his upper thigh.

The mail arriving at the church includes a twelve page newspaper with non-stop slander of faithful clergy and laity who do not line up on the editor's side in church squabbling. A shut-in, wanting communion, still grumbles about "lazy niggers" he once knew sixty years ago as a house painter. I pull into a parking place in our church lot early one spring morning and notice what I think is a fellow sleeping off a night of drinking; it turns out that he had been shot to death Mafia style and dumped in the unlocked car of one of our neighbors.

A major share of our parish budget goes into building maintenance; the mustering of concern and money for world hunger is such a struggle. Our annual bazaar draws several thousand for a day; those who respond to a series on nuclear armaments and Christian responsibility is under a hundred.

I find in my own heart a numbing sense of foreboding when traveling to a church convention I know will be ugly with the worst of passions—church fights. Martin Luther had a word for this moment: *Anfechtung*, being tested in faith and found wanting.

The litany of situations calling for grace continues, and its details are as lengthy as the entire column of humans on earth in all time past and present and yet to come. *"Whatever Became of Sin?"* a prominent psychiatrist asked in a book title a decade ago.[1] Being honest with oneself and living in the community of a congregation ought to make that question anything but hypothetical. Sin and temptation are present each day, to be exposed by the law, so that all of us who fall flat on our faces and bring others down with us can be daily lifted and renewed in what our baptism gives us: the gospel.

Recipients of grace. I do not agree that sin is always more fascinating than grace and that bad news travels faster than good. The congregation is the place where I see the far more interesting and encouraging signs of people receiving grace and finding in the Good News of Christ's atoning work the solid ground for new beginnings. People let it show as recipients of grace.

An Iranian refugee stands before the congregation on the

day of his baptism and in halting English pours out the praise of God. Parents of a splendid young man whose life ended in a drowning accident write me a note a month after the funeral, telling me of the unexpected blooming of seven buds on an Easter lily which they welcomed as testimony to the Easter hope that Christ's resurrection proclaims.

An educator comes through a season of depression so severe on occasions he can barely get out of bed. But he keeps on coming through a year's series of counsel, prayer, working at it, and persevering until the depression lifts. He depended upon divine grace as the sustaining strength all that hard way. Another person who has traveled the way of fragile emotional and mental health for years cannot handle the experience of being at worship in crowds, but writes deeply sensitive letters revealing a whole inner world made far more humane, caring, and humor-filled than the exterior circumstances would suggest. Grace is holding that delicate balance together as the letters indicate.

Each afternoon a retired engineer puts in several hours cleaning classrooms and hallways in our parish school. No one has pushed him to such a schedule; it is his way of letting grace in the heart find outlets in service. A wife whose husband suffered shellshock in World War II goes every Sunday after service the hour's drive to the veteran's hospital, where he can't always remember her name; grace keeps that woman caring for her husband and mindful of the gift of her own clear mind and healthy body.

The teenage boy mentioned above recovers from the gunshot wound in his thigh, and through the grace of Christ heals other, deeper wounds in his soul and mind and is on his way toward the future with hope. Each Wednesday a housewife makes time for a morning of volunteer work in the church office and each Wednesday evening she's back for choir rehearsal—a schedule she has kept for twenty-five years. Her alto voice and her indefatigable spirit of service are continuing testimonies to grace.

A young medical student and his fiancee come in with a different agenda than most: she can't say yes to his proposal until he comes to terms with occasional flashes of heat in the region of his heart, an eerie glow that surrounds his face

and eyes, and a dreaded experience of demonic possession
which comes upon him. Weeks later, after repeated sessions
of explicit centering on the victory of Christ over powers of
darkness into which we cannot fully probe, grace has done
its work. A shaken couple has new ground on which to build
life together.

A polio victim gets to church for prayer for her estranged
husband without becoming a victim of bitterness, and knows
where that freedom from retaliation and self-pity is found
in the forgiving mercy of God.

The woman whose self-definition is as a worthless whore
finds One who does not let her settle into her promiscuity
forever, but offers grace and gives her new openings into the
future as one who is entirely known and entirely forgiven.
And the husband who could not lift up his head in the presence
of the wife he battered is learning to lift his head and face
a new future with the self-understanding that grace provides
and the strength to let go of his self-hatred through prayer
instead of with his fists.

A man subjected to torture in a Cuban prison for twenty-
two years survives the ordeal with the grace of Christ in his
heart toward those who tried to break his spirit by means
of torture. A whole congregation pours out love and good
will for the organist and choir master who has served for
thirty-three years in a ministry of exemplary excellence. The
grace of Christ is at the heart of all those years of singing.

Every sunrise, every rainfall, every sign of life in nature
is in its own way a testament to grace. But where that testimony is found above all is in the lives of people. Whole life-
times are made new in that grace; the congregation is a place
to see it happening.

The renewal of life.   Sanctification is the church word often
used over the centuries to refer to the lifelong process of renewal. Justification, which refers to God's work in Christ for
our redemption, does not hinge on what we do. Sanctification
is the indwelling life of the Spirit, enabling us to join in partnership with God with every ounce of our energy and will
and talent.

Older parishioners can witness to the renewal of life in
its most tested times. Contrary to the philosophy of our

youth-loving culture which shunts older people aside, the congregation is a marvelous display of counter culture in its honor and care for aged members.

When a ninety-four-year-old woman who is in church every Sunday, and who can still read the hymn verses, reaches a birthday it is time to have her stand, accept her cheery wave, and applaud her heartily. She began life on the Dakota prairies. She can remember the day when her father walked out on the family. She took her turn at farming chores at the side of a heroic mother, baby-sitting the younger ones in the family with a shotgun across her lap in case rattlesnakes got into the yard.

She married an Italian-born U.S. soldier and faced with him all that a German Lutheran bride had to weather in an Italian ghetto of Chicago. She raised their four daughters in the faith, stood by her family in days of heartache as well as rejoicing, laid her husband to rest, and can still outlast her great-grandchildren at pinochle until the late hours of the night.

At so many turns along her way of life there could have been detours and bypaths in directions which deny the faith. Instead, her life has been renewed and renewing at those crossroads. Her witness has made an impact on many younger people who find themselves uncertain at the junctions of life she has passed through in faith. In a time when a great many Christians are hearing of people reborn, she helps us see that the Christian is born again and again, and that renewal of life occurs during our whole span of years, not only in a transforming moment.

Congregations have been central in the resettlement of several millions of refugees from Southeast Asia since the Vietnamese war. Each congregation that opens its heart to people seeking the freedom to live is renewed in that experience and witnesses to the renewing power of God that helps people across enormous cultural and spiritual barriers. Sometimes it appears in the baptism of several dozen people who have welcomed into their lives the Christ who makes all things new. In more frequent instances, it is an individual here, a family there, who find the gospel that which makes them new and strong under the continuing hardships of prejudice, a puzzling new culture, mastering new job skills, learning a new language and new ways, and bearing the burden of separation from family members still in political prison at home.

Alcoholism is an old but continuing backdrop of woe against which the renewed life stands out clearly. Drug abuse is a newer but even more ominous problem against which renewed life is contrasted. The men and women who have come through that wasteland have so much to tell, and their story of renewed life under God is always the story of the interdependence of personal renewal with the continuing importance of not going it alone.

The congregation is the place where such renewal is never to be looked down upon; their voice of witness is a powerful word to all the rest of us who are potential alcoholics or family members of one who shall suffer this disease of body and spirit. When it happens that someone comes to me with his alcoholic or drug addiction, the main help for him comes from fellow parishioners who know the affliction personally and who can minister to new partners out of the renewal of their own lives.

On the morning of the funeral of a member who died suddenly in his thirty-third year, a man of similar age called me at home. In a few sentences he laid out for me the remarkable similarity of his life to that of his friend whom we were about to bury. He had grown up in an upper middle-class family, completed college, entered a lucrative job, married, divorced, adopted the life style of so many caught in the tight web of the laid-back life of casual drugs, increasing alcoholism, and slavelike concern with every cultural fad. Then it all turned around for him, in the experience of repentance and the renewal of his life in Jesus Christ the Lord.

He had not seen his friend for a year, but less than a month before, he had come through town and the two men went out for dinner. What was amusing to each was the way in which both began to set the direction of the conversation toward the subject of spiritual renewal. They got there, each telling the remarkable account of coming from a life of spiritual drift, into Christ and the community of his people. The entire evening—over four hours at the restaurant table—was not enough time to cover each one's amazing story. Now one renewed life had come to its goal while the other journeys on. My phone caller was present at the service in which the homily included his sterling testimony. In all likelihood I shall have only this single occasion to meet this young man for he lives in a distant city. But that brief time together is time I will not forget; it has on it the stamp of renewal.

Acts of love. In Wordsworth's celebrated line citing the "little, nameless, unremembered acts of kindness and love" as the best portion of a good man's life, there is a truth that does not appear little or remain unremembered as people share grace. In an emergency room of a hospital where a woman's husband had died minutes before, I saw a nurse gently embrace the woman who stood there in the shock of her spouse's death. No words, just an embrace that carried its message of love. Perhaps the nurse does not remember it now; the widow does, and will continue to cherish it all her days.

The children of a family celebrating their thirty-fifth wedding anniversary let me in on the surprise event because they needed to borrow tables and chairs from the church for the backyard party. It came off with marvelous verve, an act of love which left both parents and children wondering who enjoyed it most.

Weddings and funerals are occasions when families realize as rarely before the capacity for kindness and the tangible acts of love which smooth the way. A man who knew flying and had access to a plane traveled twice to a remote north-woods location to bring in family members when a father died suddenly. Our parish hall is regularly the scene of a dinner for the family and friends returning from the cemetery. Those who volunteer food and serve it beautifully do something that can never be duplicated in even the finest restaurant: care for heartsore people with tangible acts of love. Such meals are a first step in healing.

An act of love can be a genuine word of welcome at the narthex door as strangers enter, a sincere word of greeting in Christ as the peace is passed in the communion liturgy, a hymnal shared with one who is new to all this singing and speaking together. Are people so greeted at a theater? Are handshakes exchanged at the seventh inning stretch? On buses and trains coming to and from work does someone share a newspaper? More than we realize, the acts of love in a congregation are uncommon experiences. What may become commonplace to us is not common.

For years I have begun each sermon with the greeting, "Dear Friends in Christ." Once a Korean doctor told me how much those four words meant to him. "You called me your friend," he exclaimed with an appreciation that I needed to realize anew. These acts of love go on day in, day out, in uncounted numbers. What we are privileged to see is only a fraction of them. But each act of love seen is one multiplied in its blessing. And the measure of Christianity is still this: "Behold how they love one another."

Growth in grace. It is hard to cite anything of greater significance in a congregation than the response of adults to opportunities for growth. In this sense, growth in grace means planned endeavor to enlarge and enrich the minds and spirits of believers. Our tradition has put much emphasis on the nurturing of children. We have had to learn the importance of nurturing spiritual growth in adults. More than we realized before, adults want to grow. They need the opportunity and challenge of meaningful, biblically based, relevant-to-life courses offered at times accessible to their schedules.

One useful experience has been a Sunday afternoon and evening seminar on a single subject. The sessions are completed in two hours in the afternoon and an hour and a half in the evening, with a potluck supper in between. Genesis 1–11, the biblical prophets, the birth and passion narratives of Christ in the Gospels, selected epistles, and prayer life from the Psalms have been among more recent course offerings. The Christian Lifestyle, Medicine, Healing and the Faith Traditions, Women and Men in Christ, Parenting and the Faith, Christ and Daily Work, Redemption and Contemporary Themes in Literature, The Church and the Nuclear Arms Race, and Marriage Among Christians are other courses that aim at specific interest areas for people within and outside the congregation.

But growth in grace is much broader than a parish curriculum, and it occurs in many ways beyond participating in classes. Staying at it in a shaky marriage instead of giving up too soon in divorce is a growth experience.

A college junior preparing for medicine spent a summer as a volunteer in medical missions in India and Nepal. As he put it he has "packed several years of experience into several weeks' time." The firsthand contact with Christians and life in the Third World at this formative time in his life is an acceleration of growth in all he has believed and learned from his baptism onward.

People grow in grace as they wait in faith for healing to come, for employment to be found, for failures to be accepted as God's prodding in another direction. Growth in grace occurs as people bear witness to Christ's kingdom to those who stand outside it, especially at the workplace, the campus, the neighborhood, and the family.

The growth pattern is not steadily onward and upward. When it is two steps back before the next step forward is taken, the jagged line looks patternless. But that is the pattern. The two backward steps may cover three or thirty years. As a child of four I didn't quite understand why my father suddenly stopped going to church. It was, as I later understood, because he had been refused the sacrament while kneeling at the altar in anticipation—because he had joined a labor union. The pastor saw that as rebellion against God's order, in this case a management that worked their bread salesmen up to eighty hours a week. That experience so offended the man that it took him three years to re-enter congregational worship. I've always wondered what the pastor learned from his bungling of the matter.

I cherish the memory of a man who returned to active Christian life thirty years after he took leave—for reasons which he never chose to discuss. Through those years his wife did not nag. But neither did she let his indifference stop her faithful participation in the congregation. He did come back. It happened in connection with visits to his printing business as we had work to give him. From time to time the invitation was simply stated: "Harry, the Lord has room for you and we want you in the congregation." One day he started the way back.

A mystery surrounds this. We are witnesses, no more and no less. I believe that the Lord puts long lapses to purposes we cannot fully see. But one of the things we need to see, if even through a glass darkly, is that careless discipleship on our part has a serious fallout on others. It is better to remain humble before that fact than carping at those who still stand outside.

Suffering. To minister to people with long-term pain and disability is to be in the presence of giants of the faith. An older woman has known one of the most severe of all pains; it is the disease of trygeminal neuralgia that attacks the facial and head nervous system and can drive the victim mad. She is a slight person, of gentle disposition, but tougher than steel when it comes to bearing pain. There is no logic to this experience, as though it could be seen as an aftermath of faithless living. Her message through it all is the repetition of St. Paul's statement: "My strength is made perfect in weakness" (2 Cor. 12:9). She doesn't have to say a word to those who know her sturdiness of faith, so long tested by pain. She preaches by her very existence.

Suffering has been the thorough teacher of people fooled by their own pretensions of invulnerability. It has taught people to live by grace instead of works. It has been the crucible in which gentleness has been formed in a person all-too-quick to judge others less successful or productive. It has brought people to prayer, and caused new spiritual priorities to be honored at last. And yet it must also be said that suffering can and does bring madness, despair, bitterness, and selfishness.

Why does one move toward wholeness through suffering, and another to oblivion? The mystery remains, just as suffering itself is a mystery. The only clue we have is that God has taken suffering to his own heart, as the cross of his Son reveals.

Influence. "I never knew how to give money as a sign of living faith until I began helping in the counting room at church and saw with my own eyes what some of our members give." The woman who told me that, a highly capable person who holds a major position of financial responsibility in her work, was talking about the influence one Christian can have on another.

I don't know of a better way for financial stewardship to be learned than the way she learned it. But everyone cannot count the offerings, and the idea of publishing the contributions of every member is totally unacceptable. One Christian is a template for another in the way and the words of prayer.

People come out of their fears and frustrations as widows and widowers because they see the example of others who have had it harder still coming through in care for others and their forthrightness in getting on with their own lives.

People put off investing themselves in the mission and nurture of the congregation, but what moves them is not the preacher's words. It is the sight of another, who may be much busier, rolling up the sleeves and getting into the work.

Influence has its best effect when least consciously offered. It is because of the love of God for his own sake, and delight in his work for its service to others, that people of faith become influential. Their message is not that they can change the whole world, but that the world has not changed them.

Our faith is centered in the Person of our Lord who became human for our sake. Should it be any surprise then, that he should present himself and bring us under his sway through the influence of people who are his handiwork? The congregation is the setting in which people come into contact and stay in the contact with each other long enough and in enough depth to be influential. It offers opportunities that are not to be found elsewhere.

Victories.   Victories of faith do not mean always winning as that is usually defined. Victories are the welcome outcroppings of grace, the surprises of the Spirit when the case seemed settled against us, the quiet outcome of faith over unbelief. My predecessor in the pastorate had a long, hard battle with cancer before his death. When it was clear that he would not get back home from the hospital, when he and all of us with him realized that he would not set foot again inside the church building he loved and worked so hard to build, he told me something I shall not forget. Referring to the congregation and its future he said, "The best days for Grace Church are yet to come." He would not live to see those days. He would not be present to lend his enormous store of talents to the people. But he spoke as one who never lost sight of Whose the congregation was and is and shall ever be. Such a sentence is a victory because it points so clearly to Christ the Victor.

Several times each year people are invited to a series of Sunday morning classes for adults on the basics of the faith.

It is always made clear that attendance for thirteen or fourteen weeks does not mean automatic entrance into the congregation against the will of the person. At the end of each series, I meet with the men and women one by one. Whenever a person says, in some way or another, "I want to be a part of all I have seen and heard," it is a moment of rejoicing. A victory is on display as a person heretofore standing on the sideline or walking the other way, falls into step with Christ under his banner and with his people.

Pastors need to have sharp eyes for the victories that look piddling from the outside. A terribly insecure person accepts an invitation to join a fellowship group in the parish. An embittered individual stops hating the world and joins a food pantry crew working with a sister congregation in a poverty area. One who believed for years that only his denomination would be present in heaven learns to recognize Christ's people across man-made organizational boundaries. A courageous man or woman takes leave of life in the peace of Christ. All these victories are occurring all the time while the world around us is blind to them. But they continue and will continue until time is no more.

Furthermore, we share in them. I was not sure what was going to happen when two brothers, business partners for years, found me as their arbiter in their determination to divide the business fairly. I am inexperienced in such matters. But they did not come to me for business expertise. They came for shepherding through a situation in which they needed their sanctified selves to prevail over their sinful natures. It took some hours, but it worked.

I thought the victory was over when they shook hands, and included me in the bear hug that engulfed us all three. But not quite. The brother entering retirement invited me for a fine luncheon together with his brother. Following dessert he ushered me around the corner and to the second floor of an adjoining building, where a tailor was waiting to measure me out for the finest suit I have ever owned or will ever own. Every time I put it on I remember the occasion and smile. Victories are to be enjoyed.

▸ *8* ◂

The Art of Telling a Story

EVERYONE CAN TELL A STORY, BUT NOT EVERYONE is Isaac Bashevis Singer. Greatness in the art of telling the story of people in the light of faith is not given to everyone who preaches; yet none of us can give up trying. There is much about this art that can be learned if only we give it the attention it deserves.

The Bible itself is our best teacher. Here, particularly in the Old Testament, we find the greatest people-stories in all of literature. One need think only of the matchless stories of the patriarchs, Saul and David, and Elijah and Elisha, to begin to see the art of telling stories for our times. People are not glorified in the Bible so that we see only their heroic stature. People are presented honestly, revealing greatness and baseness. They are fully human without every last detail of their existence sketched out. Literary critics, equipped with a profound grasp of the original language and varied literary style of the Hebrew Scriptures, expand our appreciation for subtle things too easily overlooked in reading the stories of the Bible: thematic key-words, recurrent actions, the function of the narrator, and the ultimate goal toward which all biblical narrative moves—the dialogue between humans and God. But the point of the biblical narration which centers upon humans as the object of God's relentless quest is more than literary. Robert Alter says it well:

The Biblical writers fashion their personages with a complicated, sometimes alluring, often fiercely insistent individuality
because it is in the stubbornness of human individuality that
each man and woman encounters God or ignores Him, responds
to or resists Him.[1]

We meet such people in the biblical narrative in a manner
sufficient for the first and main requisite of telling a people-
story in preaching—the story concerns me. Stories centered
on people must have accessibility. The style of narrating may
vary but the point of the stories is ever this: "For whatever
was written in former days was written for our instruction,
that by steadfastness and by the encouragement of the Scriptures we might have hope" (Rom. 15:4).

The final measure of the effectiveness of a people-story is
that the hearer makes the inner connection between the story
and her life. When the mind listens and says, "It's about me,"
the communication line is open. If stories about people fail
at this point, then the main thing is lost and precious sermon
time is wasted. Or worse, the hearer is defeated by regarding
the great things happening to others as only for others. Thus
gaps, not crosswalks of meaning, are created.

The art of tilting people-stories toward the "about me" goal
involves subtlety. Nowhere in the Bible is a story woven into
the text with a red flag waving: "Now listen, this story about
Jacob's wrestling with the angel all night at Jabbok is really
about you. . . ." The divine Author behind these biblical stories treats us all with greater respect than such pedantry sug-
gests. The stories have their connecting points in their
directness, honesty, and humaneness and in their linkage with
what God himself is doing with people throughout the whole
of the story. The genius of artful people-stories lies in their
simplicity, their capacity to capture moments that are so trans-
parently meaningful that everyone who hears can find involvement.

Such a grace-filled moment came to a man who was in
the midst of a marital crisis. His wife had wearied of his
years of insensitivity. He was temporarily separated from her,
living in a second floor room in the home of an older couple,

acquaintances of his. On a February morning the troubled guest arose shortly after dawn and happened to glance out the second floor window. It was Valentine's Day. A light snow had fallen during the night—enough to put a blanket of white over the front yard. The man of the house, a physician in his 80s, had just finished shoveling the front walk and was about to return inside. But, as if prompted by an idea that popped into his mind spontaneously, he laid the shovel aside and walked onto the snow-covered yard.

With a shuffle-foot step he tramped out a huge heart in the snow. The final touch was his own first name and then his wife's, joined by the word "loves." He had stamped out a love note in the snow to his wife of sixty years. The second floor guest, who was observing it all unseen, was overcome by the simple, whimsical, beautiful expression of an old man telling his wife he loved her. It was a moment of such power that the guest had to lie down on his bed and weep in the realization that in all his own years of marriage, amidst all his own striving and accomplishing, he had never done anything close to that. It was a turning point in his interior process of repentance and looking in new directions for the power of love to heal him and his marriage.

Such a story, taken out of the life experience of a Christian on a snowy winter morning, has its own handles. It carries its own momentum for the mind and heart of the hearer. The only stories that we really "hear" and embrace with our whole being are those which are "for me." That might sound overly subjective or even narcissistic, but it's true. It is of prime importance that the preacher has this clearly established in his own mind as the art of people-stories is learned by practice. Every story about people must be put to this test of potential personal application, and then told with consciousness of its purpose.

It sounds obvious to say that stories used in sermons need to flow from the biblical text. But the obvious needs saying. The main reason I know why a people-story does not necessarily flow from the text is that I have begun with the story instead of with the text. That is more tempting to preachers than most realize. An experience has made an impact on the one preaching; the urge is strong to work it into the sermon whether it fits or not. A text is pushed and pulled in all directions except its own direction when that temptation prevails.

Of course, another reason why stories and texts don't fit is that the sermon ambles on without any textual basis at all. Or textual study has been slighted and the preacher tries to get by on illustrations as decoration without substance. A *New Yorker* cartoon pictures a slightly sheepish preacher leaning over the pulpit and saying: "It's been a very full week so if anyone would like to throw out a scandal, funny anecdote, or a current event, I'll wing it." There's no substitute for solid textual work. The art of telling a people-story is based there. Like all art, it possesses a discipline and an integrity of relationships.

The more one delves into textual study, the more readily the text of Scripture will yield its own links not only to what happened three days ago, but what in human life truly flows from the text. The great thing about people-stories is that they don't have to be from yesterday or last week. More often than not they ripen with age. Resting in some niche of the preacher's memory, or recorded in a page of one's own journal, or stored away in a set of file cards kept for the right text coming along, the passage and the story are joined together one day. The time this might take is not time lost.

What flows from the text may be a people-reference that is only a phrase or a sentence long. Such brief allusions are the fruit of highly disciplined sermon work before hand. Few of us can craft a story in a single sentence. In this connection one marvels at Jesus' skill in giving us five single-sentence people-stories within the space of one chapter (Matt. 13:31–34, 44–49). To appreciate such things, one need only sit down and try to write five distinctive stories of a single sentence each. More commonly, the people-story that flows from the text is a paragraph rather than a sentence. I have had to learn the art of trimming down too much preface to the story itself. The hearer does not need to know all that I know about the person in the story. A sentence or two at the most must suffice for setting the context of the story. Otherwise the connection between the text and the story gets lost too easily, and the hearer forgets what this story being told is intended to illumine.

The art of telling stories is best practiced as the preacher gets out of the way of the text and story connection. It clutters the way when the preacher falls into the habit of saying, "This point reminds me of a story." That's needless. The point is not that the preacher is reminded. The point is in the story itself. Conversely, an artfully told story moves onto the screen of the mind with the hearer hardly noticing its appearance. The preacher takes us from the substance of a text to the substance of its meaning in a person's life without unnecessary intrusions.

There is, then, a rhythm in this art. It comes with the discipline of careful rhetoric and practiced economy of words to make sure that the hearer is led smoothly and cleanly into the story. Our Lord is our teacher, as Luke the evangelist tells it when Jesus meets a man who had trouble with the question of who was his neighbor. With one graceful stroke of language Jesus has the man's attention and is leading him into the truth through this story: "A man went down from Jerusalem to Jericho and fell among thieves . . ." (Luke 10:30). When a potential follower who was a man of great wealth heard Jesus' invitation to sell all his goods and give his wealth to the poor, he faltered and turned away. In an instant Jesus made the point to his own followers, who could no doubt identify with the crestfallen hesitator: "How hard it will be for those who have riches to enter the kingdom of God. It is easier for a camel to pass through the eye of a needle than for a man of wealth to enter the kingdom of God" (Mark 10:17–22, 25). The connection is immediate and forceful. The hearer is not lost in clutter or trivia.

The essence of rhythm is that it has not only a smooth beginning as it flows from the text or from the central point of the sermon; it has a steady movement to a climax and an ending that helps the hearer to move on with the rest of the sermon. A story needs to build, not to a shouted climax, but to one in which the preacher is fully involved. Cute little asides have the same bothersome effect as needless and repeated parentheses in written sentences. Animation, intensity, empathy, and the preacher's own passionate concern for meaning belong in the building of the people-story. Some people do this with a firm, even tone. Others cannot help but match the content of the story as it moves with a changing pitch of voice, facial expression, and movement of arms and body. Whatever is natural to the person is appropriate to the expression of meaning.

Recently I sat in a congregation of Kenyan Christians in the southwestern bush region of that African nation. The preacher personified the voices of different people upon whose lives he was drawing. Although I do not understand the Luhya tribal language he was speaking, I could grasp something of the meaning he was imparting. The packed room of Christians, most of them barefoot and cash poor, were rich in their response to the story. Their involvement in its meaning came through in their own body movements and voice affirmations. Are we in the western world too caught up in formality? Can our own black American congregations teach us much about how to hear a story and how a story can be told? Undoubtedly so. But each congregation has its own style and whatever works for the effective communicating of the truth in the lives of hearers is what counts.

Some black preachers can build a people-story for twenty minutes or longer, without anyone in the congregation looking at a watch. That is not my gift or style. Nor will it fit the listening span of those who hear me preach. A crisp event out of a life experience can move dramatically to its point, even in a shorter story. For example, the following comes from Abraham Lincoln's pathway to the presidency. (The text of the sermon is 2 Corinthians 6:9, where Paul describes a life that is "struck down but not destroyed.")

Failed in business in 1831.
Defeated for Legislature in 1832.
Second failure in business in 1833.
Suffered nervous breakdown in 1836.
Defeated for Speaker in 1838.
Defeated for Elector in 1840.
Defeated for Congress in 1843.
Defeated for Congress in 1848.
Defeated for Senate in 1855.

Defeated for Vice President in 1856.
Defeated for Senate in 1858.
Elected President of the United States in 1860.

—Anonymous

Defeat after defeat, but then the climactic breakthrough! The account can hardly be rattled off as if reading telephone numbers. Something astonishing and noteworthy breaks in upon the hearer's mind as the last line comes through. That is the moment to lead directly to the purpose for which the story is used in the sermon. The stage is set for the hearer to realize the "for me" character of the story. God brings surprises. His grace is ever breaking in upon people as an unexpected gift, an undeserved favor. When there is no reason to hope, and all the lights have gone out over the western horizon, then comes the dawning of grace with its newness and hopefulness. We are defeated by job loss, classroom failures, repudiated proposals, business disasters, by the pernicious duration of disease, the death of one so close, the waning of cultures and the demise of whole civilizations. But inside all these inevitable events another history is running its course, the saving history that enters our own story of life as grace is given us and channeled through us to others.

The art of telling a story trains hearers not to listen as though they already knew the outcome. Jesus kept his audience off balance with his stories that featured the hated Samaritan, as the one grateful leper who turned back with thankful praise for being healed. Who would have expected the shadow of the cross at the climax of Jesus' parable of the father who kept sending faithful messengers to the murderous tenants who kept doing them in? "Surely they will listen to my son whom I shall send. . . ." And the listener was ready to nod assent, looking for a happy ending. But the Son is the victim whom they murder in cold blood. That came as a surprise and an offense to those who heard.

People-reference in preaching is not always with happy endings. The Bible teaches us to be pessimistic about man, optimistic about God, and therefore hopeful for the future. People living in the real world know better than to take Pollyanna tales as the way of the cross to which Jesus calls us. Yet people who live lives conformed to the cross of Christ are not despondent, but carry us in Christian realism through their own life story to an understanding of what is really going on in our own lives and the purpose God has in them. That awareness can dawn upon a person through another's actual experiencing of the cost of discipleship. The dramatic tautness of the story carries through to its goal in the hearer's mind because its substance is costly, not cheap grace.

Thus the art of telling stories of people is not the same as telling success stories. The New Testament does not shield us from Judas or Pilate—or the brutality of the Herods. But these life stories are in the Gospels because Jesus came to *this* fallen world and not some other, unburdened by sin. The point of these stories, and their counterparts which must be heard in our preaching from time to time, is that we have One who has been tested in all things as we are, yet without sinning (Heb. 4:15). The dark side of life experiences cannot completely blindside us when we get the "for me" point of lives that have faced the worst. A warning comes to us; the critical seriousness of our plight comes through. The least the hearer can conclude from such moments in preaching is that the preacher is dealing with things as they are. And the most that can come from such moments is the hopeful word of the cross that can fall on the soil of a truly seeking heart.

The art of lifting up people in preaching keeps one conscious of the economy of such references. Here the rule applies that more is not always better. My own years of preaching have taught me that one solid reference is often enough—two at the most. There is no rule determining the placement of the reference in the homily. My friends who listen and give me helpful critique seem to agree that most frequently I place them toward the latter part of the sermon. Any place can work. Sometimes the sermon begins with that illustration, sometimes it comes at mid-point through a quotation from a letter written. Sometimes the whole point of the text is reiterated in the concluding story of one who illumines it faithfully.

Finally, the art of telling stories of people is the skill of setting the truth in the best of all perspectives—human life under the truth of God. Perspective is the gift which keeps us from giving up too soon, from going on in the wrong direction, from blindness to life's dark side of mystery, and from ever selling short the surprising power of God's grace. The First Epistle of John is magnificent in its perspective. The lust of the flesh, the lust of the eyes, and the pride of life—these things and all that is not of the Father pass away. But the one who does the will of God abides forever (1 John 2:16–17).

The primacy of love and the abiding mercy of the God who supports us and all things in his redeeming love is the perspective that we need to set other priorities back in their place and put first things first. A great deal of what irks us daily and gains so much of our attention and energy doesn't deserve it. Perspective gives us a grip on what does count and lets us release the rest of it. That gift may be missed in sermons which hover over the heads of people hungering for it but never finding it in sermons that founder in sterile, impersonal rambling or dogmatizing. Peopling the gospel story can bring that perspective home in ways that nourish the heart and reset the spiritual vision that has been blurred. Christ Jesus died and rose again so that the preached gospel might bring his vision to ours and his fullness to our waiting hearts.

♦9♦

Toward Change and Growth

INDIVIDUALS CHANGE AND GROW AS THE WORD DOES its work. The same is true of congregations. The aim of preaching is to proclaim the redeeming work of God through his Son to the end that growth in Christlikeness takes place—in individuals and in the community of the faithful.

Preacher and congregation do well to heed the key role of preaching in that process—not only the formal act of preaching in the worship assembly, but also the preaching that takes place as the whole community of believers speaks in faith and acts together in love within its own fellowship and toward the world. Preaching brings awareness of the need for change and the goals of growth that are derived from the biblical message. Preaching must also supply motivation and provide access to the means for growth in the parish at large.

The way in which a congregation becomes a mirror to itself and to other congregations is seen clearly in the first letter of St. Paul to the congregation at Corinth. The need for change is so clearly proclaimed, as the technicolor sins of these fledgling Christians are lifted up for all to see. But no less earnestly does the pastor/apostle keep on pressing home to the Corinthians "the more excellent way." The love of Christ that is theirs in the gospel is the motive for changing and growing. For through the gospel people bear, believe, hope, and endure all things. The Corinthian letter is instructive also in its witness to the partnership of pastor and people in the changing and growing that come about as the Word of God takes root in the lives of people. .

Seasoned Christians have said that congregations cannot grow if preachers are not growing. I think that is very nearly the truth, but I prefer to say that congregations can hardly grow if the preacher never gets off dead center. When the pastoral leadership in the congregation is motivated for growth and clear-headed about how and where the congregation itself provides opportunity for growth, the whole place is that much more exciting and alive day after day.

The first day I arrived on the scene as the newly graduated seminarian ready for ordination in the congregation I still serve, the pastor met me upon arrival, chatted with me in friendly conversation along the way to the church building, and then sat down with me in his study to get serious about the ministry there and my relation to it.

"Dean, I want to emphasize one thing as far as you are concerned . . . ," he said. I thought I knew what would follow: a courteous but firm reminder to me that seminary graduation does not insure instant wisdom for ministry, that things had been going quite acceptably before I arrived, that I had best lay low and say little until I had lived my way into the congregational way of life. Nothing of the sort. He fixed his eye steadily on me and said: "We're not doing everything around here as best as the Lord would have it done. So, whatever you see that we don't see, whatever gift you bring among us that we do not possess, pitch in! We need you and want you and are anxious to grow with you as you learn and grow with us. . . ."

Such a beginning floored me. Three decades later in the same congregation I still am awed by the sheer gift of being a pastor to people who respond heartily to the collegial way of ministry. Otto Geiseman rests in Christ's peace now, but his opening sentence to me in his study—confirmed so many times by the realities of collegial ministry in the half-dozen years I served with him—has been a model for me.

If it is with pastoral colleagues and other fulltime staff people that one serves, that emphasis can hardly be overstated. Each new colleague brings some gift, possesses some charisma, is the recipient of some particular talent and insight that must be entered into the full flow of service to people. People are quick to pick up on that spirit and grow with it. One common means of growth on the part of those who preach is enrollment in further study in academic institutions or in selected course work that buttresses specific areas in which the preacher is mindful of his own gaps. Such planned growth is exemplary.

The explosion of Doctor of Ministry programs in the graduate schools of American seminaries in the past fifteen years is a good sign. Clergy realize that faithful ministry does not consist of tanking up during the seminary years and coasting the rest of the way. A learned ministry is not coterminous with intellectual airs of superiority; it is one aspect of loving God with our whole mind as well as our spirit and body.

Classroom work is not the main resource for change and growth in and with the parish. The congregation itself is. People who love God and care deeply for his church have insight and the motives and skills to put them to work toward growth for all in the congregation.

Two widows in their early 60s let me know of their sense of being a fifth wheel in much of the congregational apparatus for fellowship and service. Older single adults are among the last to be thought of when it comes to the congregation planning for their continued growth as they live through radical changes in their lives. These two persons saw that more clearly than I, and were instrumental in the formation of a fellowship group that has filled the lonelier weekend hours for hundreds of widows, widowers, and older single adults during the years since. Their ways of mutual ministry within and beyond the fellowship group has encouraged us all. Their witness has found its way into many sermons. By being who they are and doing the works of faith and love together, they have helped the entire congregation to grow and to be blessed in such a change.

Several years ago it was suggested that we have a Sunday potluck for anyone and everyone who had any idea for congregational growth. That was the price of admission—one idea on something that we were not now doing but ought to consider doing. It was a lively group of several dozen people who attended, and very interesting to see who did come and what ideas were brought with them.

One young woman took her turn in the circle of idea-telling

to remark on the smaller clusters of church members that offered opportunity on a regular-gathering basis for people to get to know each other, pray together, study Scripture together, size up local parish and/or neighborhood needs more effectively, and deepen in the experience of belonging together. After all the other idea-bringers had been heard and the assembled group came to consensus on which idea seemed most urgent for the good of the whole parish, the cluster plan was an easy first.

Thus an idea was launched that held promise for change and growth. It traveled the regular route of presentation and discussion in the leadership channels of the congregation, but with one critical flaw. The person who launched it was not invited to keep it going through subsequent channels. I took that job on; instead of being the support person to foster the one who advocated it on the basis of her experience in another congregation, I became the presenter. Perhaps that was one reason why that promising idea for change and growth has not yet really taken hold. It is now in some stage of incubation/reincarnation/failure/reappearance in altered form. It suffered the fate of too many promising ideas for growth in the congregation—appearing to come more from the top down (if that is the appropriate metaphor for the clergy) rather than coming up from the member(s) who know its value and are ready to participate.

The growth we experienced through the initial failure of an idea was of the kind that is so hard to recognize because of its very obviousness. The entire congregation does not grow at once. Any idea, regardless of its merit, needs time, a base among those ready for it, *careful nurturing of adequate leadership to enact it,* and openness to the changed format the idea can take in order to be appropriate to the particular congregation. Our parish did not respond to the neighborhood proximity standard of what will bring and keep people together in a cluster group. Our people seemed more puzzled than helped by the borrowing of a Greek New Testament term, *koinonia,* as the name of the enterprise.

Our people helped us see that better preparation of leadership was called for. The awkwardness and resulting hesitancy about prayer and growth in the Word among ten or fifteen laity gathered in the host's living room told me much about the growth needs at deeper spiritual levels. In our case, 1,800 people, who live in nearly thirty-five differing suburban communities, who have cars to go everywhere, television sets to keep them at home, who are part of the maceration of life into isolated individualism in a large American urban sprawl, didn't change or grow much through an idea that seemed so ripe for us when we heard it and pictured it in our minds.

In an interesting contrast, the African catechist who explained to me how the rural parish of 11,000 Kenyan Christians works, spoke of more successful cluster groups there. There is no paved road, no car, no electricity in the three- to four-mile radius of this parish. Christians here gather at least twice each week in the cluster of grass-thatched huts that are no more than a few minutes' walk from each other. Each small community has its leadership; they gather regularly under the catechist's leadership and take news of the parish, prayer, Scripture, admonition to reconciliation of parishioners at odds with one another, plan ways of preparing to meet the inevitable famine period that comes each March/April, and other things which have to do with the daily life of faith.

If one of us from the West is minded to call such Christians "the younger churches," we had better be clear about our own youthfulness and our own need to learn from Christians there. Certainly the external circumstances have much to do with the functional community that springs up everywhere in this land where the *harambee* (Swahili for "let's pull together") spirit abounds. Yes, these human beings would find their ways of belonging complicated by all the gadgetry and distracting consumer comforts that make it so easy for us in the West to think we can get along without each other, and to assume that the Christian religion joins us to Christ but not to each other in any sense that makes for change and growth.

It is not clear how the change and growth will occur in our own congregation in this regard. But we are changing and growing. Changes come slowly, the kinds that truly have depth and lasting power. Growth takes place in congregations according to needs and goals appropriate to the uniqueness of each.

The dimension of depth is the most significant measure

of spiritual growth, individually and in congregations. South America, Africa, and South Korea are places in today's world where Christians are growing fastest by statistical measure. But that is not the same as depth. Christians and congregations in the hard mission areas of northern Europe and our own cities in the United States must not be defeated by declining numbers. The church growth movement is not evaluated by head-counting. Depth of growth has to do with the practice of the faith in the daily vocation.

I have seen nonchurched people pay tribute to the depth of a Christian's ministry in his job. The man had just retired. He could no longer be instrumental in letting contracts to a host of suppliers through his influential executive position in one of America's largest companies. But the people he had dealt with year in and year out gathered from around the country to honor him as his retirement began. They invited me to attend. One after another they spoke of how it used to be, before our member occupied the position. His predecessor, they explained, could be counted on to connive, to manipulate, to be unashamedly false to his word. His idea of business dealings featured lavish dinners that, more often than not, turned into drunken extravaganzas with the hotel furniture in shambles by the early hours before dawn.

Then Gus Baehr came along. Things changed. Suppliers did not always get the contracts they hoped he would grant. But his integrity, fair-dealing, trustworthy words, and an occasional business lunch or dinner that never deteriorated into an orgy were appreciated. Mr. Baehr made a short speech of appreciation to those who gathered. He made it clear that his worship on Sunday carried over into his life on Monday. His words were an expression of the kind of depth that never gets measured in church statistics. But such depth is the fruit of being a part of the Christian community that gathers for the Word and disperses to do that Word in the world each week.

Such a testimony from one member of the congregation finds its way into pulpit proclamation, and the whole congregation has an occasion for growth. Should such moments never find a voice? Are not such people immensely helpful toward growth in spiritual depth for all who face the realities of the daily job? The depth dimension of change and growth has to do with how and why Christians become people of prayer, of grateful hearts for blessings given, of persistence in discipleship in the face of opposition.

Growth cannot occur without change. At the congregational level, seeing and doing new things come about as people and pastor see and do together that which contributes toward edifying change and spiritual growth.

Again, the people-to-pastor-to-pulpit chain of events is so significant. This was driven home to us during a time when the economy forced several of our people out of work. Joblessness is a threat to every person able to work; to lose a job is to instinctively feel a threat to one's personhood. When people of the congregation spoke of what that trauma meant in their lives and their families, it was time to sound the invitation through a sermon to everyone who had no work or who had ever lost a job to come together on a weeknight evening to see what happened. The fifteen or so who responded included people now jobless as well as those who had gone through it.

It was a remarkable evening, the first in a series of weekly meetings for mutual support that have followed in the year since. I had thought the prime need of men and women now out of work was specific leads and strategies for finding a new job. Not so. As numbers of parishioners present pointed out, the first thing to be changed is the idea that the loss of job is the equivalent of personal failure. One man told of how he had lost four jobs in the course of his years, and on each occasion he was not the problem, the business itself was. But he had to get beyond the dead-center point that everything collapsed because of him. Each person then jobless was immediately responsive; and the work of mutual ministry and support has gone on for members and jobless people outside the parish as well.

Such a support group, widely known in many parishes across the land, was a new experience for us. It exists because people in the congregation send signals for help. Nor could we have imagined that the key leadership person in the continuing support group would be a young woman in her late twenties who has enormous capacities for hearing out people and staying with them in enlightened care. That's the kind of change that lifts an entire congregation and moves us forward. Just to know that such mutual ministry takes place, without ever personally taking part, is a leaven for good as the story gets out through preaching and other forms of parish communication.

Change in forms of worship is a specially perilous process. Any congregation that has ever adopted a new hymnal knows, or ought to know, that the path between adopting by majority vote and adapting to the new reality is filled with pitfalls. Every congregation is comprised of people who forget or never had occasion to realize that the previous generation of worshipers who took on the present hymnal when *it* was new and forbidding had their share of problems with it. The path toward change in this area is to be traversed with prayer and fasting on the part of those who lead the way!

In this instance our experience has been much more heartening than humbling. Without assuming that all the people are pleased all the time with all the newness in liturgy or hymnody, we started out—with some fear and trembling in the face of the inevitable ruckus that accompanies just the sight of a new book of worship in the pews. Three years later, we're beginning to be at home with liturgies that do expand our spiritual horizon. Because we have had people gifted in church music and patient with all the parish, including those who were just beginning to get the hang of the *old* hymns (a generous number of which appear in the new hymnal), we have been changing and growing. There have been a handful who have simply balked and won't join in the worship of God because the new book is there. This takes place in a time when Christians are hung and shot in South Africa, tortured in Cuba and Ethiopia, and arrested and jailed for public worship in Nepal. But if balking at a new hymnal will work as well as persecution and tyranny, the devil doesn't seem to mind.

Women now participate in the larger ministry of the congregation. Is that change a response to the feminist movement more than a careful hearing of Galatians 3? Or is it in some way a response to both? The latter seems more the case, as we work hard to see together the mysterious ways of the

Spirit in all the channels through which he is pleased to work. And to what end is the change in this case? Not for its own sake, nor as a repudiation of our forebears. But congregational change toward a more inclusive ministry opens up the ever wider range of gifts that God bestows. When that is clearly the purpose of change, and when its goal is the enlargement of the mission of the congregation, then change is not faddism. It has substance and it is going to continue.

We have learned something else about the significance of people in the process of change toward greater spiritual growth. As parish leadership changes through regular intervals of service in elected or volunteer positions, more and more people are called upon to contribute their experience and insight toward growth. Stories of the same person who has been the church treasurer or Sunday school superintendent for forty years are stories of many other people denied. Revolving leadership promises greater freshness and a wider swath of people contributing their best toward edifying growth through purposeful change.

Two more aspects of parish change and growth belong here.

One is stewardship of money. Why do we either shy away from it or become obsessed with it? As the Gospels abundantly testify, Jesus was at home on the subject. His grace doesn't fail us here as we must tread where angels cannot enter because they neither earn salaries nor keep bank accounts. Once again the main point of this chapter is relevant: people in the congregation can move the parish toward greater faithfulness in giving.

We had gone along with modest salary adjustments through the zooming inflationary line of the past decade. Then a member of sound faith and a firm sense of stewardship simply stated that our congregation was not beginning to reach its potential in giving. We needed to change and the change needed to begin with more challenging goals and more trust in the power of God to motivate us. And so, in a year of considerable economic pressure, the people took on a 20 percent increase in the parish budget.

The goal was set by parish consensus. The increase was clearly the initiative of laity. Our people recognized that we were blessed far beyond the record of our giving. The people to be served by increased giving were kept in view. Not every aspect of the parish budget was increased at once. The step-at-a-time process was more digestible. The preaching throughout the ensuing year stayed centered upon the boundless giving of God. More and more, spiritual life and parish participation was the groundwork for the increased giving. That goal was reached. All felt grateful and happy. No single person or group of givers pulled up the slack alone. Such change occurred because a youthful member saw the matter more clearly than any of us and helped us grow. Prayer, preaching, and worship respond to that insight. Through a few, the Spirit of God does so much for the many.

Another aspect of parish change concerns mission. Like every other congregation of the church universal, we need constantly to learn anew the truth that the people of Christ exist for the sake of those not yet a part of his people. How does this mission take form in the late twentieth century? In myriad ways. But our particular experience, and the changes we have passed through in mission, are evident at this point. Worship is the heart of mission. When people with no commitment to Christ's grace and lordship come into a service of worship, they are exposed to a dynamic to which we can only bear witness as a sign of the presence of the living Christ. More than any other single facet of congregational life, worship centers the mission of the people.

Each congregation has some particular gift or trait, or set of them, that marks it out as an arm of mission to the surrounding community or to another part of the world. In our case, a Christian school is one of those gifts to us. Hard work goes into making the school very good at what it does.

Another aspect of our parish mission is the presentation of a series of Bach cantatas each year over the past dozen years. Doing that one thing, and doing it well, our choirs and instrumentalists and their leaders are part of a unique mission. Recovering and celebrating that magnificent heritage through a congregation (J. S. Bach wrote all his cantatas for presentation in a congregation at worship) has meant outreach to numerous people whom we would not otherwise reach. Couples come to our door seeking marriage; so often they are without faith commitment and each such opportunity for ministry is mission.

The same is true in ministry to people who are hospitalized or in times of bereavement; mission goes on as people are reached who have come to know their need of God as never before. Each year many of our members travel abroad in business or as students or tourists. We're only beginning to recognize the potential such traffic has for enlarging our sense of mission and our partnership with Christians near and far in speaking and doing the truth that saves.

Change and growth take place because God is gracious and puts into the minds and hearts of his people the Holy Spirit, who never lets us sit still. Seeing his work in people of the congregation and joining them in the kind of change and growth that lifts up his glory may be painful at times and marked by setbacks. But the grace is there to keep us moving, and it is heaven on earth to be a part of it.

♦ *10* ♦

Yes, You Can Do It

Too OFTEN, WE WHO PREACH SUFFER A MALADY that can be described as the tall-steeple virus. The illusion is that the small congregation is somehow less than those larger assemblies of Christians who gather under imposing brick and mortar. The virus can turn up in this form when it comes to people in preaching: "Those who preach to 2,000 have it better than those of us who are happy if 80 are present on Sunday." This chapter is an appeal to everyone who preaches to answer the question, "Can I put people in preaching effectively?" with an unqualified Yes, regardless of the size of the congregation.

A musician isn't better because she plays a dozen pianos instead of one; the mastery comes through one pair of hands on one set of keys which strike one set of strings for the music to flow. Does the fact that a surgeon is affiliated at three hospitals make him proficient? Isn't the skill derived from patient-by-patient operations, with everything in his head and hands concentrated on that one patient before him on the surgical table?

The size of the congregation is not the key to effective sermons. It lies in the eye and heart of the one who preaches. Indeed, a case might be made that faithful work concentrated on two hundred or fewer Christians in a congregation stands a better chance of quality than those who at best can be a chaplain to 2,000 or more people, and pastorally close to no more than forty or fifty at a time. The size and situations of congregations will inevitably vary, but whether they are large or small in number, every one in the pastoral calling is on equal ground when each one keeps to people in preaching.

How many priests or ministers serving large, urban congregations can draw upon an experience like this? A strapping, Lake Michigan-wise fisherman started up his snowmobile on a January morning with the thermometer hovering around twenty below. Another fishing partner on a second snowmobile went just behind him. The two headed into a stiff, northerly wind several miles from shore. Their island home is just off the northeast tip of Wisconsin in Lake Michigan waters.

Walter knew the perils of checking fishing nets in winter when traveling by snowmobile over the ice. The path he always took could support a Mack truck. But by some quirk an underwater eddy of warmer water had weakened a patch of ice where it was least expected. In an instant Walt and his machine plunged through mushy ice into 34-degree water that was 180 feet deep. His heavy boots and snowmobile suit were like an anchor dragging him under. While his partner's machine sailed into the same ice hole, barely missing the man struggling for his life, the other man threw himself off onto the thicker ice. In doing so, he was soaked by the thin layer of water sloshed up as Walter broke the thinner ice back with his elbows until it was thick enough to hold him from being swept under the ice by the lake current.

Gordie, the partner, spread-eagled himself face down on the ice edge and reached Walt's outstretched arm. But the 230-pound man in a water-soaked suit nearly pulled Gordie in with him, insuring the death of both. By the good Lord's help, as Walter later put it, he told Gordie to stop pulling and stay flat on the ice edge as a thirty-five-mile-an-hour north wind blew at him.

Both men knew that a human can survive four minutes at the most in water that frigid. With less than a minute left until Walter would have been numbed into fatal unconsciousness *Gordie's soaked suit froze to the thicker ice surface*, giving him enough grounding to pull his partner to safety. The two shaken men walked back alive to tell their story.

And their experience, by their own testimony a work of divine providence, found its way into a sermon on the Ephesians 2 text which speaks of the grounding God lays for the church, with Christ Jesus the chief cornerstone. Hearers make vivid connections with that incredible people-story which can apply the point of the Pauline text. The congregation of which Walter is a member is what church statisticians would classify as small. But look at the resources that are there! How many tall-steeple preachers have access to such people-experiences?

Here is the point reiterated from less Arctic surroundings. It is another people-experience from the ministry of a most gifted young pastor and writer, Walter Wangerin, Jr. His reflections on what he learned while ministering to a black woman in her final days of life are moving and instructive:

> In the second year of my ministry at Grace, Joselyn Fields fell sick. In spring they diagnosed a cancer. In summer they discovered it had metastasized dramatically. By autumn she was dying. She was forty-seven years old.
>
> Spring, summer, and autumn, I visited the woman.
>
> For much of that time I was a fool and right fearful to sit beside her, but I visited her.
>
> Well, I didn't know what to say, nor did I understand what I had the *right* to say. I wore out the Psalms; they were safe. I prayed often that the Lord's will be done, scared to tell him, or Joselyn, what his will ought to be; and scared of his will anyway.
>
> One day when she awoke from surgery, I determined to be cheerful, to bring life unto her and surely to avoid the spectre that unsettled me—death.
>
> I spoke brightly of the sunlight outside, vigorously of the tennis I had played that morning, sweetly of the flowers, hopefully of the day when she would sit again at the organ, reading music during the sermon. . . .
>
> But Joselyn raised a black, bony finger, pointed squarely at my nose, and said, "Shut up!"
>
> I learned so slowly in The City. Yet so patiently The City—and Joselyn Fields—taught me. I, who had thought to give her the world she didn't have, was in fact taking away the only world she *did* have. I had been canceling her serious, noble, faithful, and dignified dance with death.
>
> I shut up. I learned. I kept visiting her. I earned my citizenship. And then the autumn whitened into winter, and Joselyn

became no more than bones, her rich skin turned ashy, her breath filled the room with a close odor which ever thereafter has meant dying to my nostrils. And the day came when I had nothing, absolutely nothing to say to my Joselyn.

This is as true as the fact that once my face had burned.

I entered her room at noon, saying nothing. I sat beside her through the afternoon, until the sun had slanted into darkness, saying nothing. She lay awake, her eyelids paper-thin and closed, drooping, watchful eyes—saying nothing. The evening took us, and with the evening came the Holy Spirit. For the words I finally said were not my own.

I turned to my Joselyn. I opened my mouth and spoke as a pastor. I spoke, too, as a human. More than that, I spoke as a man to a woman.

I said, "I love you."

And Joselyn opened her eyes. She put out her arms as a parishioner, I suppose; as a woman, to be sure. And she hugged me. And I hugged those dying bones.

She whispered, "I love you, too."

And that was all we said. But that was the power from on high, cloaking both of us in astonished simplicity, even as Jesus had said it would! For in a word that I did not know I knew, a need had found not only its expression, but its solution, too!

Joselyn died. And I did not grieve.[1]

Whether large or small, the congregation yields an unending harvest of rich experiences that call for a voice in preaching. As we pray for the gift of eyes of love for people which can see these things, we learn that a marriage healed, a long-prayed-for breakthrough to faith experienced, an aged parent cared for, a child nurtured to spiritual maturity, a visit with a parishioner on the job, a hearing out of a soul struggling faithfully against formidable odds, all involve people offering up that which is so preachable.

Those who minister in larger congregations have the task of keeping individuals in clear focus as great numbers of people are part of the whole ministry of the congregation. If it is a multiple staff situation, there is something greater to look for than administrative efficiency. What are the stories of people that each one gleans from the respective sectors of ministerial responsibility? How can staff meetings be more than routine paper shuffling? These abound in mutual enrichment as the best of each one's ministry to and with people is part of the ongoing agenda.

The benefits are multiplied as each has opportunity to pass along to others the witness which comes through the sharing in which all participate. That is not a random happening. The best mark of leadership in a large staff serving a big congregation is that all eyes are opened and all are made aware of how much their experience with people in ministry means for the good of the whole.

In my own experience, that takes place most frequently in regular sessions of worship by the staff. We set aside an early hour on a weekday morning, and while the one leading is free to choose the format for worship, the occasions which seem to stand out in my mind are those in which "reporting in" takes place. People get better and better at seeing significance in their own rounds of particular ministry as they hear with benefit the witness of another. It might take some time for this to become natural and really exciting for a group of people who have differing gifts and tasks, but it is worth the time it takes. Such things can't be forced. Patience is required. But each one does have something to give to the colleagues that only that person can give. Best that it not stop there but bring blessing to others.

When children, at the conclusion of a Sunday school series or a youth confirmation training period, are asked what helped them most, their answers invariably come out as, "The stories you told us. . . ." That's hardly surprising. The truth of God is meant for life, and the people-experiences which mirror his life in ours are the best ways we learn and grow, regardless of our age.

If the question is, "But can I do it?" let the answer be learned in the actual doing of it. People in preaching is meant for every preacher. There is no such thing as a congregation that can't offer people-experience to the preacher. Wherever even two or three are gathered in Christ's name, he is present. And that is enough to make things happen that are rooted in time with an importance that stretches into eternity.

♦ *11* ♦

Endings

CHILDREN IN OUR FAMILY AND IN OUR CONGREGATION occasionally take time to prod me into listening to a rock group that's currently "in." One thing I've learned about these songs is how frequently their endings fade out into inaudibility. It's up to the listener to decide if the thing has actually stopped. "Is the song over now?" I keep asking.

Sermons need endings that ought not prompt that question (or the other kind: "When *is* this thing going to end?"). It can be a central point reiterated. A series of outline-highlights summarized briefly can underline the central point. Perhaps a people-experience simply referred to in a concluding phrase pulls the whole sermon together. Sermon endings vary, but sermons need clear and convincing conclusions. My predecessor ended his sermons with this sentence: "May the peace of God which passes all understanding keep your hearts and minds in Christ Jesus." Hearing him preach over several years, that ending sentence never became trite. For all of us who heard him gladly it was a reminder of the bridge between the Word preached and our faith lived.

Endings that are a question or a challenge to the hearer also have their place, for preaching is an appeal to people for changed lives under God. Asking if a biblical text will be taken seriously can secure the text rather than making it a threat. The one preaching often says the Amen to the sermon, but shouldn't the congregation also say it? If that immensely important word is to be spoken by the congregation (with the understanding that those who are not yet ready to do the truth proclaimed should not say the "Yes, it shall be so"), the hearing of sermons can take on more depth. Good preaching calls for crisp, clear endings. Good sermons are about one thing at a time, secured by the conclusion of the homily.

How often it happens, to me at least, that thirty seconds after the sermon ends and the congregation rises to sing a response, some point forgotten pops into the preacher's mind. Unless it is the announcement that the building is on fire any sermonic P.S. is to be avoided like the plague. This is an important moment for the hearer. The biblical text is beginning its work of translation from hearing to doing. It must not be interrupted by a "There's one more thing. . . ." Sermon conclusions that are really endings are connecting points to other actions of worship.

One of the unique rewards of preaching is the end of a preaching day. For most of us that is Sunday. Whatever the day of preaching, there is something special about its ending. Martin Luther used to go from the castle church in Wittenberg a few hundred yards up the street to his house to enjoy a glass of ale "while the Word did its work." Regardless of how one views preachers and ale-drinking, Luther's practice points to something of the sense of peace and full enjoyment of the sheer joy and privilege of preaching the gospel. Time with family or friends, time to relax and rest for at least half the Sabbath, is precious time for preachers.

Part of what the preaching day's end enjoyment is about is doubtless the satisfaction that work has been done and now it's time to rest. But the greater satisfaction lies in the work the Spirit is graciously beginning, now that the gospel has fallen like seed into human hearts. The contented, satisfying, fulfilling day's end for the preacher is all of that because the week following will bring continuities for those who hear and those who preach.

Blue Monday? Not really. The key is that the preacher believes the Word preached is the ministry-creating Word that is going to carry everybody ahead with hope. Harried Saturday, perhaps. But not Blue Monday. The ending of the preaching day is sanctified with an inner peace, and prayers of thanks for the wonder of such a calling.

Ministries also come to an end. The one who preaches is assigned to or called by another congregation. Robert Raines tells of a minister somewhere in the midwest who had been a burden on a congregation for over twenty years. One Sunday morning he startled the long-suffering congregation with this closing sentence of his sermon: "The Jesus who called me here twenty-three years ago is the same Jesus who is now calling me on to another pastorate." No wonder the choir arose to sing, "What a Friend We Have in Jesus"!

A minister in a congregation not far from ours terminated a lengthy pastorate by taking the church council off-guard at the end of a regular meeting of the group. He simply said, "I have decided to leave." He got up and left. The people thought he meant he was closing the meeting. In fact he was leaving that congregation. Keeping congregations guessing like that, or leaving them startled or confused, is a form of ministerial peevishness. It must signify the final overflow of resentments nursed for a long time.

The saddest story of a pastorate's ending came to me from a young friend, a seminarian, who was helping out a congregation. On *Easter morning* the preacher told the people he was preaching his farewell sermon. It consisted of a rambling list of his frustrations, disappointments and hangups during his years as a minister. The resurrection of Jesus Christ was not mentioned. Not once. One hears of such things and wants to weep and marvel that congregations can ever survive such episodes.

Happier endings of ministries abound. A young minister preached a farewell sermon that was thoughtful, faithful, and encouraging, mirroring to the congregation the ways the people had ministered to him. That sermon is still remembered by many who heard it. When purposeful ministries come to an end, either through retirement or moving to another place of service, a momentous opportunity is at hand for all present to realize anew the towering sufficiency of Christ to keep his people as change occurs. It is an occasion for preacher and people to celebrate one more time the love which has upheld them all along.

The ending of an active pastorate is a deep mixture of grati-
tude and penitence, joy and sadness, hope and wondering
about "what now?" But as far as the preaching content of
those partings is concerned, it is best done when the "for
us" power of the gospel is clearly proclaimed. The preacher
can leave with that uppermost in the lives of people and be
sure that they will keep on hearing as a new proclaimer comes
along.

And finally, for the preacher as well as for all, life has its
ending. We die only once, and there is no practice for it in
the final measure. Our death may or may not be heroic. It
may come in the early stages of a promising career, or at
our very peak, when we are at our mature best. To some is
given the gift of an ending that is abundant in the love and
affirmation of an entire congregation, and years of continuing
enjoyment of service with the lighter load of retirement time.

In most of the instances that I can think of, retired clergy
actively seek some way to continue in ministry that is com-
mensurate with their energies. It may be in pastoring a smaller
congregation without a pastor for a time. More often it is in
being available to preach occasionally, to visit among the sick
or shut-in, or to be of help wherever a congregation finds a
niche for the retiree. That is a significant thing. It indicates
that a minister or priest continues in some way in a vocation.

People have retired from jobs with the wish never to have
another day's involvement in that type of work. The same
can happen to clergy, of course. But it is rare that a man or
woman does not retire from the ministry actively seeking and
welcoming a lightened load in the same work. More and more
clergy are able to retire in these times without being forced
by economic reasons to remain fulltime in ministry long beyond their capacity. One reason is improved retirement plans
in congregations and denominations. Another reason is the
increased number of clergy spouses who have worked, saved,
and helped make it possible to get along on a retirement in-
come. That is a trend which will increase, and it is welcome.
Retired clergy are a sterling resource for congregations. Most
of us want to die with our cassocks on. The ideal we envision
is not the rocking chair, but a Bible class or sick bed or occasional pulpit where we can still be with people in ministry.

But die we must. Our lives, too, come to an ending. We have only one such ending after our last sermon is preached, our last Sabbath enjoyed, our concluding retirement year completed.

Our death itself may or may not be heroic. There is nothing in our vocation that insures that we who stood by so many others in their death will be stoic or lyrical in that concluding journey. Death may claim us at the peak of our best years of service, or cut it all short before the ministry is well begun. However and whenever the preacher's life ends, the last, best thing in death is the gospel that has sustained him all along. Then people who have so often been a part of his preaching come with their ministry and consolation. It is all by grace. We are ever beggars, and never is that so clear as in the moment when all must be left behind except the one thing needful— the dear, holy cross through which we are delivered from death into the realm of life and immortality.

Until then, we preach, in season and out of season, in urban places as well as the countryside, to believers as well as unbelievers, among the seasoned doers of the Word as well as those only beginning, under Gothic steeples as well as in storefront missions, to young and old, black, brown, and white, men and women—we preach. We keep on preaching "as unknown and yet well known . . . as poor, yet making many rich, as having nothing and yet possessing all things" (2 Cor. 6:9–10). Our place in the long and noble procession of witnesses and martyrs, apostles and prophets, is all too brief. But each day is a gift, and each person a treasure.

Viewed in that light, our brief span is not cheerless or futile because of its brevity. Our place in the line is given meaning and made bright because of the Christ who calls us. He gives us himself to proclaim in his Word. He surrounds us with so many lives that are proclamatory. Preaching his gospel through sermons rich in reference to the life experiences of the faithful is our high calling. It is second to none on earth.

Footnotes

Chapter 1

1. C.S. Lewis, *The Weight of Glory* (New York: Macmillan, 1949), p. 15.

Chapter 4

1. Arndt Halvorson, *Authentic Preaching* (Minneapolis: Augsburg Publishing Co., 1982), p. 121.

Chapter 5

1. Alan Paton, *Too Late the Phalarope* (New York: Charles Scribner's Son, 1953), p. 153.

Chapter 6

1. Michel Quoist, *Prayers* (New York: Andrews McMeel Parker, 1963), pp. 61–63). Used by permission of Sheed and Ward, 115 E. Armour Blvd., P.O. Box 281, Kansas City, MO 64141–0281.

Chapter 7

1. Karl Menninger, *Whatever Became of Sin?* (New York: E.P. Dutton Co., 1973).

Chapter 8

1. Robert Alter, *The Art of Biblical Narrative* (New York: Basic Books, 1981), p. 189.

Chapter 10

1. Walter Wangerin, Jr., *Ragman and Other Cries of Faith* (San Francisco: Harper and Row, Publishers, 1984), pp. 62–64.

Recommended Reading

Aycock, Don M., ed. *Heralds to a New Age.* Elgin, IL: Brethren Press, 1985.

Bartow, Charles L. *The Preaching Moment.* Nashville: Abingdon, 1980.

Claypool, John, *Glad Reunion: Meeting Ourselves in the Lives of Bible Men and Women.* Waco, TX: Word Books, Publisher, 1985.

Cox, James W., ed. *Biblical Preaching.* Philadelphia: The Westminster Press, 1983.

_____. *Preaching.* San Francisco: Harper & Row, 1985.

Erwin, Gayle D. *The Jesus Style.* Waco, TX: Word Books, Publisher, 1983.

Fresh Ideas for Preaching, Worship & Evangelism. Waco, TX: Word Books, Publisher, with Christianity Today, 1984.

Killinger, John. *Fundamentals of Preaching.* Philadelphia: Fortress Press, 1984.

McKenna, David. *The Psychology of Jesus: The Dynamics of Christian Wholeness.* Waco, TX: Word Books, Publisher, 1977.

Robinson, Haddon. *Biblical Preaching.* Grand Rapids: Baker Book House, 1980.

Shelley, Marshall. *Well-Intentioned Dragons: Dealing with Problem People in the Church.* Waco, TX: Word Books, Publisher, with Christianity Today, 1985.

Wardlaw, Don M. *Preaching Biblically.* Philadelphia: The Westminster Press, 1983.

Willimon, William H. *Preaching and Leading Worship.* Philadelphia: The Westminster Press, 1984.

Index

127